SEOUL GIRL

an autobiography

Ann Baron

SEOUL GIRL is an autobiography. Names, places and incidents either are products of the author's memory and some names may be changed to protect the privacy of the person.

No part of this book may be reproduced, stored in a retrieval system, or transmitted by any means without the written permission of the author.

Copyright @2021 by Ann Baron

Cover by Ann Baron & J.S. Earls

Edited by Mike Baron

Design & format by J.S. Earls

Introduction

Folks have asked me what the purpose was for writing this autobiography. When I turned 60 years old this gave me pause to reflect on my life. How can I inspire others? How can others learn from my mistakes? What is it like growing up as an adoptee and in a multicultural family? What it is like growing up in a mostly white society and being one of a few minorities in my city. How to see the signs of an abusive person and not get ensnared in an abusive relationship. What can I give to others in wisdom and lessons learned?

As I started sharing with others what it is like being adopted, this began many conversations with others about adoption. I thought that I was doing this for myself but I found that the conversation generated on this topic gathered more interest than I realized.

My story will hopefully give insight to others who are adopted or have adopted. I may never know why I was given up as a baby. Yet, I feel my life has a plan and a purpose. God had me in His hands and has showered me with His protection and blessings. For this I will be eternally grateful.

1

The Beginning
ABANDONED

THE WARMTH OF THE COLORADO SUN comes through the windows as I savor my morning coffee with my loving husband and puppies around me. I have a good life. Going back over 60 years, a small, scrawny baby was left at the front door of THE Holt Adoption Agency many miles away in crowded Seoul, South Korea. That fragile baby hanging on to a thread of life was named Adela Kim. And this is my journey from South Korea to America. From feeling Abandoned to feeling Loved.

The story began before I was born, with the Korean War in the 1950's. During that time many babies were born out of wedlock or were left orphans due to the war. A couple named Harry and Bertha Holt were touched and moved by the stories out of South Korea of many homeless babies. Traveling to Korea and seeing the huge need for families for these children, they started an orphanage called Holt Adoption.

I was born on June 10, 1960. The Holts started these orphanages with their own money and in war torn places, where many abandoned babies died. God had His hand in my life and I not only survived but I flourished. There was a plan and a purpose for my life that would unfold through the years. The huge blessing showered on me by God would not completely sink in until I became an adult.

In those days international adoption was rare, especially adopting multiple children. The Holts successfully had a billed passed in Congress allowing multiple adoptions, which opened the path to our family and many others adopting more than one child from a foreign country. God was already making the way for our family to come together.

Those first four years in the Orphanage are with me still. In some ways it seems like a dream, or another person's life far away and across many miles. I remember days of hunger and secretly stashing food under my pillow. I was hungry every day. To this day I still have insecurity about never having enough food to eat. I still stash candy or snacks in my purse to have on hand at all times. Looking back on my baby pictures, I was a tiny, thin little girl. My files said I would be cute once I filled out more.

I remember couples coming to the orphanage and leaving without me, filling me with sadness that I was bypassed. I had a heart murmur and tested TB positive therefore, I was hard to place. This is why I spent four years in the orphanage.

We did outdoor swings and play time. I remember playing on the swings. As my swing reached the top I looked out over the orphanage, past the wall to the apartments and skyscrapers in the distance, I didn't feel unhappy but the orphanage was very restrictive. It was not a home. We were kept in our cribs at night and only allowed to go to the bathroom if we called for one of the helpers there to come get us.

LESSONS LEARNED: Sometimes you can have a rough start in live but that doesn't dictate the rest of your life.

2

Orphanage Years
HOW TO COPE & LEARNING TO WAIT

MY DAYS AT THE ORPHANAGE were spent mostly in my crib. But on occasion we would go outside and play on the swings. I remember singing children's Korean songs such as *"Nabiya"* which means "Butterfly" in Korean. I recall standing outside and singing this sweet song with the other children. I loved singing and still do though only in the privacy of my own home. *"Nabiya's"* lyrics are "Butterfly, butterfly come fly, fly, Yellow butterfly, white butterfly come here while dancing. Petals dance in the breeze too, Smiling, smiling and laughing. The sparrows tweet, tweet, tweet, Singing while dancing."

That scarcity of those early years still cling to me like a ghost whispering that I will never have enough food.

I remember when couples would come into the orphanage but leave without me. Wondering when my forever parents would adopt me. Since, I had a heart murmur and was TB positive I was a "hard to adopt." I lingered in the orphanage for four years. Even as a very young child knew I did not have my very own parents and would search the eyes of every adult that entered the Orphanage to see if they would be the one. I was constantly disappointed when they would leave without me. Time passed and I was potty trained and already walking. Still no parents to whisk me home to a loving family.

I remember swinging on the play equipment outside and having fun. But still it haunted me that at near four years of age I did not have a home of my own or parents to love me.

LESSONS LEARNED: The early years affect you for your entire life. Always feeling hungry as a child still influences me to this day. Understand why you feel deprived but don't let it control you.

3

To America

THEN ONE DAY, the orphanage prepared me to fly on an airplane to San Francisco, California. I did not understand what was happening at the time, that I was going to my new home in America. Each part of the trip delighted me from being on this huge plane to flight attendants waiting on me. Such fun! In my mind I did not grasp what was happening or how drastically my life was going to change. Every morsel of food was tantalizing to my taste buds since I was used to oatmeal and rice almost every day. Seeing the bright, cheery smiles of the flight attendants waiting on me hand and foot was such a novelty. I felt like I had gone to heaven and savored every minute of the trip.

After what seemed like an eternity, we landed in San Francisco in the huge, noisy airport to meet my new parents, Von and Betty Brenner. My four year old mind had no idea exactly what was happening. Later on, my Mom said that I was in a corner of the room talking to myself. I always was a talker. The Holt volunteer introduced me to my new parents and I went with them wearing a dress which engulfed my tiny body. My new mom had a crisp, blue dress that fit perfectly. They took me to my new home in Eugene, Oregon.

LESSONS LEARNED: There is a family out there who wants and loves you. It took four long years but I finally had a family of my own.

4

My New Family

WE DROVE UP to a perfectly manicured yard and a green, one story house. My parents brought me home to their comfortable home in Eugene. My parents showed me a pink and brightly colored room. My own room! The bed was a frilly and soft with a pretty doll on the pillow. I had been used to living in a crowded room with many other orphans. There was my very own rocking chair and toys waiting for me.

That first night at my new home, I yelled and yelled for my Mom to come to my room and let me use the bathroom. I was trained to not get out of bed unless someone came to get me. Mom gently explained to me that I did not need to call for her and I can get up whenever I wanted too. Who knew!? A newfound freedom.

There were little creatures crawling in my thin, stringy hair. Lice! One of the first things my Mom needed to do was remove the lice out of my hair. She cleaned my hair and made sure the lice were killed and removed. I had no idea that having lice in your hair was a problem!

Mom asked if I wanted to go shopping with her and I was excited. I had never gone shopping. Mom took me to a big department store where I lost sight of Mom. Fear gripped me. Huge tears began rolling down my cheeks as I shrieked for mom. I
was petrified that I would never find my Mom again and be alone. After that incident, I stuck closely to Mom. The fear of being lost and not finding my parents haunted me for years.

Since my English was not very good, Mom patiently taught me how to say words. We sat on a comfy couch and read nursery rhymes out loud for me to hear how to say the words. To this day some words are still hard for me to say. Likely, I had learned some English in the orphanage but not much.

LESSONS LEARNED: Even if you cannot see someone it doesn't mean that you are lost. Security comes from being loved and wanted.

5

Adjusting to America

I WOULD OFTEN WAKE UP SCREAMING due to horrible nightmares. Each time the nightmares were the same. A monster popped out of a car as I was walking by. Another recurring nightmare was being at a store and losing my mom. My eyes would search the vast area looking for Mom. In my nightmares I cried hysterically and yelled "mom, mom" to find her. Usually, I would wake up and realize it was a bad dream. These nightmares lingered for years.

One evening we were all in the living room watching TV. Mom and Dad put on their coats and headed toward the door. This was the very first time both of my parents had left the house together. I was left with my two older brothers. Paul was my parents' only biological child, eight years older than I. He was tall and gangly, a teenager with glasses. Jim, two years older and stocky, had also been adopted from South Korea.

My brothers were occupied watching TV when I bolted for the front door, with my legs running as fast as I could to go after my parents. Fortunately, my brothers ran faster than I did. My big fear was that my parents would never return. The effects of living as an orphan for the first four years left me with an indelible fear of being abandoned again. Later, we would laugh about this incident but at the time, I was scared about losing my parents again.

Another memorable event was being baptized. My mom was bathing me and poured water over my head and she explained to me that I was going to be baptized with water. At the time, I did not understand the reason for the baptism, only that was important to my parents. It was years later before I understood the importance.

In Kindergarten I did not have very good English. My teacher kept me in the "dunce corner" most of the year. Sadly, I sat in the corner by myself, not interacting with anyone else. I cried every day. This was probably the way for the teacher of dealing with me since I didn't speak English. To this day I never told my parents about this.

LESSONS LEARNED: People may not understand you and they deal with it the best way they can. Folks aren't rude but simply curious.

6

Medical Conditions

THE REASON IT TOOK ALMOST FOUR YEARS for me to get adopted was because I was hard to place due to underlying health conditions. I had a heart murmur and I am TB positive. Sometimes, I wonder how my life would be if I was adopted as an infant and came to America at a much earlier age. Yet, each experience makes up who I am. Fortunately, nothing ever came of either medical condition. For the first few years that I was in America, I had to have a chest X-ray every year. This was to make sure that TB had not become an illness in my body. This has never affected my life. The heart murmur may have gone away or it has not become a threat to me either. I am thankful that I have had a full and healthy life.

LESSONS LEARNED: The "hard to place" children can still have a wonderful life. Don't let limitations stop you.

7

What Are You? Brown Outside, White Inside

MY WHOLE LIFE there has been this juxtaposition between being brown on the outside but feeling white on the inside. This feeling is hard to explain. Complete strangers would come up to me and ask me where I was from and my nationality. This never happened to my white brother Paul. As a child, it did not seem odd or out of the ordinary because it happened so frequently. In later years, I realized this was not normal.

When, I was six years old my mom threw me a big birthday party. My girlfriends were invited over and I wore a frilly, blue dress. The taste of the sweet birthday cake, friends chattering and gifts still make this a highlight of my childhood. One of my gifts was my very first Barbie doll and thus began my love for dolls. The Barbie doll had fair skin and was blonde. This began shaping my image of what is beauty. You needed to be thin, blonde and white. Not until I was ten years old did I get a doll that was brown skinned.

When I was out in public with my Mom, complete strangers would come up to my Mom and ask her if I was her child. Also, a common question is "what are you?" What they were meaning was what race or country did we come from. Folks were simply curious and I thought that was normal until I was older and realized my white friends did not get asked these same questions.

One time we were at a grocery store with Mom trailing like little ducklings. A stranger pointed at us kids and then asked Mom about us. They wanted to know where we were from and if we were her kids. Mom, without skipping a beat, answered that they take after their Father. This made me laugh because our Dad was white too. Mom finally got fed up with all the questions and thought that would stop them.

I often wonder how my parents must have felt, having adopted kids of a different race. It was very unusual in those days. Mom may have felt singled out or constantly under scrutiny. My folks were older parents and perhaps folks thought we were their grandchildren. It must have been awkward.

One bright day, I walked by a store window and caught a glimpse of my reflection, I wondered who that person was in the mirror. Then, I realized it was me! I was shocked to see that black haired, almond shaped eyes person staring back at me. On the inside I felt blonde and white, but, on the outside I was dark complected. The external persona and the internal persona did not match. This took me many years to reconcile.

When almost everyone you look at is white, that is the image of what is "normal." All through school there were only a handful of non-white students or people on our town. You would think that Eugene, Oregon being a University town, would have more diversity. But, in those days it did not.

One day my Mom asked me if I wanted to get my hair done like hers with curls and cut short. Of course, I did. I wanted to be like my Mom and fit in. Mom took my little hand into the hair salon. The stylist had me follow her back to the salon to have my hair done, but made Mom stay in another room. For a little child, this was frightening and especially since I was anxious anytime I was away from my Mom. The stylist chopped at my hair to cut it short. Then she put the tight rods with the smelly formula on my hair. She gave me a mirror and I started bawling. I came out looking like a Chia pet! My hair was cut so short with tight curls all over my head. I was horrified. My poor Mom probably felt badly and thought I would like my hair cut and permed.

For the first two years I was in America I had two older brothers. One brother was two years older and he was also adopted from Korea. His name is Jim. We were never close. My other brother is Paul and he is eight years older. Paul was my parents only biological child, since Mom could not have any other children. Since Paul was so much older than us he seemed more like another parent than an older brother.

LESSONS LEARNED: Sometimes you are different from others but that doesn't have to be bad. People out of ignorance or curiosity ask personal questions and they aren't bad people but curious. You don't have to look like everyone else to have a good self-image. Embrace being different from the crowd.

8

A Trip To Kansas
BLIND AS A BAT

MY GRANDMOTHER HAD A SEVERE STROKE and we went back to Kansas. Mom and I rode a bus from Oregon. The bus was basic and smelled of too many bodies crammed in a small space. Each night we slept in our chair with no room to stretch out. Every day, Mom gave me a box of sweet raisins which at first tasted sugary and chewy. By the time we arrived in Kansas, I was sick of raisins. To this day, I still don't like raisins.

We arrived at a hot, dusty farm in a small town in Kansas. The sun beat down on us every day. The smell of farm animals wafted into the farmhouse. I looked out on the horizon across the flat terrain for miles, so different from Oregon where the treeline blocked the view. Grandma's house was older with china cabinets and faded paint. This trip was my first out of state since I had arrived in America.

One day, my Uncle Louis took me along in his old pickup truck to feed the cattle. I rode in the truck bed. We bumped along the dirt road to the cattle. As we approached the cattle, the smell of hay and animal dung filled our nostrils. We stopped the pick-up and suddenly, these large animals come close to the truck which terrified me. A high pitched screech came out of me. My Uncle calmed me down. It seemed so sudden that I saw the cows and their huge bodies scared me. This was the first time I had ever seen cows and I did not know what these monstrous beasts were. Uncle Louis said to my mom "she needs glasses." My parents had no idea that I was "blind as a bat." This explained all the times I ran into trees and objects. My parents thought I was clumsy. My parents fitted me for eyeglasses and it changed my world. No more running into trees!

LESSONS LEARNED: Parents, if your child seems clumsy or slow then get it checked out. Make sure your child's learning skills, eyesight, hearing and motor skills are working properly. It may not be normal to keep running into walls.

9

Frilly Girl & Tomboy

OUR GRANDMA SEWED a frilly, pink, gingham dress for me. I felt so pretty wearing this beautiful dress. I wanted to play in the backyard and Mom said be careful to not tear the dress. I assured my mom that I would be very careful. Playing outside, I decided to climb over the fence. I was halfway over when I heard a rip. The dress got caught on the fence. A big tear in the dress ruined the pretty dress Grandma had made for me. I felt awful.

Growing up I always wanted to wear Mary Jane, patent leather shoes with frilly socks. I always preferred dresses to pants. Then I would sneak into my mom's cosmetic stash and try out her lipsticks. I liked anything girly.

Now, my Mom was more of a Tomboy and I didn't learn how to dress or put on makeup from my Mom. It wasn't mom's fault she simply didn't have an interest in that fashion stuff. It would take me years to learn how to put on make-up and how to dress.

LESSON LEARNED: Don't climb a fence when wearing a dress. Your parents are doing the best they can. It is okay being different from your parents and everyone is unique.

10
Focused on Food

IN GRADE SCHOOL, they had a cafeteria where we ate lunch every day. Each day I would go through the line with all the wonderful food placed on a hard, plastic tray. Then trotted off happily to cold, metal benches. What a concept that by simply going up to the food counter food was placed on my plate. Then, I would go back for seconds and thirds. The school cooks let me go back for food as many times as I wanted. Thinking back on this, usually the kids only went through the lunch line one time. The cooks probably thought that little, skinny kid needs to fatten up. Frankly, this is all that I can remember about first grade was having as much food as I wanted. All the other kids would finish up their lunch and I was always the last person still eating in the school cafeteria.

LESSONS LEARNED: The kindness of others. Thinking back on this experience I realize the school cooks were making an exception for me to eat as much food as I wanted. The earlier years deeply impact you.

11
Jon is Adopted
EXCITEMENT!!

ANOTHER BIG EVENT HAPPENED when I was six years old was the adoption of my younger brother, Jon. Jon was four years old when he was adopted by our family. He was the last child adopted by our parents. Little did they know that Jon would be the one who would take care of our Mom in her later years.

My Mom worked with Jon as she did with all of us. When Jon was in grade school a teacher wanted to put Jon on medication for ADD but my Mom refused to put him on any drugs. Thank goodness. She worked with Jon and helped him in school. Sugar was particularly bad for Jon and he would get very agitated if he had too much sugar. Our Mom was very patient.

Little did I know that he would become one of my best friends and we are still close to this day. I was now an older sister and relished having someone to "boss around" and play with. We spent many hours in our backyard building cities out of paper. We called it Marcola. We would braid twine and entertain ourselves for hours. Jon was a good friend.

Jon was also my buddy in "crime." When Mom and Dad were away from home we would sneak into the Brandy. Then, we would put in more water so the Brandy looked full. Likely, our parents knew we were doing this but they never said anything to us.

We tried mixing all of kinds of food combinations, testing what would taste good. Some combinations were great and others were awful. Soy sauce with baked potato. Mustard on a carrot.

LESSONS LEARNED: Sometimes that extra "surprise" child can be the biggest blessing in the family. Jon was a great brother and later caretaker for our Mom. Also, hide the liquor from your kids! All kidding aside, kids are curious and they will try things.

12

On TV

SITTING IN THE RED WAGON, my brother, Paul, gave a hard push. I went careening down the sidewalk and freaked out. The wagon landed sideways and I got a black eye. I arrived with this shiner and my teacher asked me if I wanted to be on TV? Sure! Sounded fun!! The educational TV channel was doing a story about a sick girl and because of my black eye they put me on TV. This was my first and last experience of being on TV. My 15 minutes of fame. They filmed the show. Later they recorded us talking separately. Another new experience.

The lady who was the host of the TV show then treated us to ice cream. I felt so special. What a fun experience and I was not afraid of the camera.

LESSONS LEARNED: Sometimes a bad situation can have a good outcome.

13

Getting Contacts
I CAN SEE CLEARLY NOW

MY MOM DROVE me to the eye doctor, an elderly man with a kind manner. He had me look into this machine and say "better" or "worse" if the letters on the wall looked clear or fuzzy. The doctor showed me how to put the small, circular lens or contacts into my eyes. I was eight years old when I got contacts. What a life changer. Not only could I see better but I felt prettier. Plus, the contacts made it easier to do activities. Over the years, I did lose a couple of contacts but for being that young I did pretty good. Now, I wasn't being called "four eyes."

LESSONS LEARNED: Sometimes a small thing like getting contacts and no longer being called "four eyes" can pump up your self-esteem. Seeing better and taking away the ugly glasses improved my self-image.

14
Birth of an Entrepreneur

ONE DAY my Dad needed a little cement for a project around the house. Our neighbor was running cement on his driveway so I knew he had cement. We had delicious plum trees in our yard. In my seven year old mind, I felt like we had a good possibility of getting the cement we needed in exchange for the juicy plums. After picking a bag of plump, purple plums I walked over to the neighbor and explained we needed a small can of cement for a project at our house. If I gave him the plums would he give us some cement? He agreed and I happily returned home with the can of cement. The beginnings of my persuasion skills. Of course, as kids you are always practicing learning how to get what you want from your parents. But in this case it was a neighbor and someone I didn't know that well. I was happy to accomplish this successful barter.

LESSONS LEARNED: You never know if they will say "yes" unless you ask. Take the risk and ask for what you want. The worse they could do is say no. Yet, the outcome can turn out positive too.

15

The Helper

IN FIRST GRADE, at the end of the day I gathered up the dirty dishes and cleaned them. My teacher never asked me to do this but I wanted to help her. At the end of the year, my teacher gave me a set of pink dishes. I was overjoyed with this special gift.

LESSONS LEARNED: Helping others is its own reward.

16

Church Camp

A HIGHLIGHT OF MY CHILDHOOD was going to summer church camp. My parents drove me to the camp which was about an hour from home. We pulled up to a woodsy area with ponds. I anticipated the fun week ahead. My favorite part of church camp was the arts and craft time. Each day we learned a new craft. A world of creativity opened up to me. We made copper embossing designs and decoupage. Each day I eagerly went to the canteen choosing any sugary candy or soda I wanted. I had a big sweet-tooth! Not good on the teeth but fun.

During our break times we would go to the swimming hole. The murky water had a sticky mud bottom. One day as I was swimming I ventured out into the deep end. Panic set in and I started flailing in the water and I almost drowned. A friend saw me in distress and she rescued me. To this day, I am fearful of deep water. Later, I did take swimming lessons but still remember that near drowning.

LESSONS LEARNED: Have experiences where you develop your creative side and learn what you are passionate about. Also, access your risk and make sure before you jump into deep water that you are ready for it.

17

Skipping School

IN GRADE SCHOOL my best friend was Sarah. We hung out during the day and did sleep overs at each other's homes. We were at school and Sarah said let's go down to the nearby grocery store and buy some candy. Anything that had to do with candy I was up for. We both skipped school to go to the local store and buy candy. Sarah and I were out on our big adventure. We knew that you were not supposed to leave the school grounds by yourself but we did anyway. Everything was going smoothly and we gleefully headed back to the school. Then a car stopped abruptly next to us and it was our teacher. She was driving back to school and she saw us. Damn, we were caught! Our teacher made us write a note to our parents explaining what we did. I begged her to not make me do this because my parents would ground me. My parents had a serious talk with me about how dangerous this was to leave school and not to do it again. I never skipped school again. When you are a kid you don't think about consequences. What if someone kidnapped or attacked us?

LESSONS LEARNED: Be aware that your actions can have consequences. Sometimes your parents do know what they are talking about.

18
Middle Child

I WAS THE MIDDLE CHILD with all brothers. As I would say to folks, I played baseball with my brothers but they wouldn't play with dolls with me. We played baseball, football and basketball. I loved to play with dolls but none of my brothers were interested. Also, I learned to accommodate and adjust to others. You learn to please others and make sure the others are happy before your own happiness. I was a people pleaser. I still want to please people but I am learning that I don't always have to make everyone happy.

LESSONS LEARNED: You don't have to make everyone happy.

19

Grade School Years

WE LIVED IN A COMFORTABLE HOME in Eugene, Oregon. It was a ranch style, one story house. Our Dad built an addition as our family grew. Every summer seedlings and small plants grew in a large garden. In late summer, we drove to nearby orchards to pick juicy, ripe peaches. We picked the perfect peach for wonderful peaches and ice cream. The highlight of my summer. We canned peaches, tomatoes and pears. Friends let us pick filberts which we roasted and then froze. My mom was a stay at home mom who made everything from scratch. My Dad was an insurance agent for State Farm Insurance. I played in our large yard with my brother, Jon, or with the kids in the neighborhood.

My parents bought a plot of land in Lapine, Oregon. All that was on the land were pine trees and bushes. Almost, every weekend we went to the lot and camped. Many hours we pulled bushes out of the land. It was tough work. Then, we would go fishing. Actually, my parents went fishing and I watched them. Putting squirmy worms on the end of a hook was not my idea of fun. Poor worms. I was always happy to eat fresh trout baked over a campfire with butter and onions. Still to this day the best fish I have ever tasted.

We crossed a murky, creek barefooted. When we came out of the creek little leaches clung to our feet and legs. I screamed! It was horrible. My Dad removed them using the butt of a lit cigarette. Eeek! Part of being out in nature.

Since, my Dad loved fishing he bought a small boat. Many weekends we headed out to Coos Bay, Oregon a small coastal town in Oregon. We would go out in the bay and cast out crab traps which held chicken carcass. Then, we would wait a while in the calm bay enjoying the sea air and sun. Dad, would round up the crab traps eagerly looking forward to the bounty of Dungeness crab. He would pull up the traps and see how many legal size, male crabs we caught. Sometimes, we would catch 30 crabs in one day. Often we shared with our neighbors since we caught so many Dungeness crabs! At the end of the day, we cleaned them and we ate them with melted butter. To this day, one of my favorite foods.

Our little house on Harris Street used to be a fruit orchard. Ripe, golden Bartlett Pears grew on the tree and we enjoyed this juicy, sweet treat each summer. Another fruit tree we had was a deep purple plum tree which bore juicy plums all summer. In the front yard, we had yellow plum trees. Since both my parents grew up on farms, we had a big garden. I loved going out and picking fresh peas off the vine. The crunchy, sweet pea was amazing. A magnificent, huge, maple tree grew in our backyard. We spent hours climbing and hanging from the branches. We composted before composting was "in." Our garden soil was a deep brown and full of nutrients. Everything my parents planted grew and flourished. After moving to Colorado later on and trying to grow a garden then I realized what rich soil we had in Oregon.

When I was in sixth grade, we learned Spanish. I would come home from school and teach my Dad the words I had learned in Spanish. He was excited to learn the new words I had learned in Spanish. Dad made me feel like I was a smart person.

LESSONS LEARNED: Enjoy the simple things in life.

20
Jap

THE SCHOOL I ATTENDED was a quiet, suburban neighborhood school. I was a quiet but a good student. One of those "nerdy" kids who studied a lot. I kept out of trouble and tried to stay under the radar.

When I went to school, some of the kids would stretch their eyelids and call me "Jap" which made me feel bad about myself. For one thing, I was not Japanese but the kids did not care to find that out. I felt like they were making fun of a feature which I could not do anything about. I could not change my eye shape. My self-confidence was torn down and I felt like an "ugly duckling." One day playing outside at the playground a boy ran me over with a bicycle and I skinned up my knee. I don't know if he ran me over because I am Asian or he was being a bratty kid. At that age, I did not know what the word "discrimination" or what it meant being a different race meant.

LESSONS LEARNED: Words can hurt and scar but you are not what people call you.

21

Trips To Kansas

OUR FAMILY LOADED UP our Buick Station Wagon with four kids and two adults. The reliable Buick pulled a small Aloha trailer behind it. All six of us would travel in these cramp quarters but we saw it as an adventure. We started out early in the morning traveling from Oregon towards Kansas. Both of my parents grew up in small, farm towns in Kansas. They still had many relatives in Kansas. We pulled up to a woodsy, KOA camp along the way and parked. It was a hot summer day and we all changed into our swimsuits and headed to the swimming pool. As we approached the swimming pool the smell of rotten eggs hit us but we still jumped into the pool. Going swimming was a luxury in those days. We headed out the next morning to our next camping point. A couple of us were at the laundromat at the camp when a huge dust storm swirled in. We made a dash for the trailer. Once in the trailer, we leaned against the wall to keep the trailer from going over. Even though it wasn't luxury accommodations there were many fond memories.

On the trips we always stopped at Yellowstone. We made a point to see the glacier, Old Faithful which sprouted out of the ground with steam and sprays of water. Spectacular. We awed at the majesty of these glaciers. Driving along through the park we spotted Bears and other wildlife. It has been many years since I have visited Yellowstone but memories I will relish the rest of my life.

Since we were city kids visiting the farm was fun. One time while we were visiting, a mama pig had a bunch of piglets. One piglet was a runt and could not fight its way to get food. The runt was tiny and cute. We hand fed the piglet and showered it with attention. Later on, I learned that the runt died. I felt sad.

There a lots of wild, feral kittens running around the farm. One day I caught the feisty, little kittens with their sharp claws. Then I dressed them up in doll clothes. I am surprised I caught them and they didn't claw the heck out of me. Poor kittens. They probably thought, oh no this child is going to make us wear these stupid clothes.

Uncle Louis brought back a small, box turtle for us as a pet. We were so excited since this is the first turtle we ever had seen. Put it into a box to keep the turtle safe. I put my hand in the turtle's box to give him water when it snap! The damn turtle had snapped onto my thumb and he would not let go. Screaming for someone to get the damn turtle off of my thumb. My family helped to detach the turtle from my finger.

LESSONS LEARNED: Go on an adventure and see new places. You will survive traveling with six people in a small camper and not kill each other. Note to self. Not all animals are pets. Also, be careful when putting your hand in a cage!

22

A Citizen at Last

I CAN STILL REMEMBER the day vividly. My mom dressed me up in a beautiful, red dress with gold buttons and white, patent leather shoes. I was 10 years old. We said the pledge of allegiance and the Judge pronounced us citizens of the United States of America. Since I was one of the younger citizens, I stood with the judge and said the Pledge of Allegiance with him. Later on we enjoyed a celebration at home. At the time, little did I realize how important this day would be. Becoming a citizen of this wonderful country and all of the blessings this country has to offer. I feel blessed.

LESSONS LEARNED: Being a citizen of the United States of America is a huge blessing. I never take this for granted and I am glad to be an American.

23

She's Not Bossy, She's Showing Leadership

IN 6TH GRADE our PE Teacher was asking the students to be quiet and listen to her for instructions. The kids continued jabbering and making noise. No one was paying attention. The teacher repeatedly asked them to listen and was ignored. By this time, I was exasperated and I loudly yelled at everyone to stop talking and listen to the teacher. Dead silence. The teacher looked at me in surprise that such a little girl could have such a big voice and everyone to listen. First time I realized that I could speak up and use my voice.

LESSON LEARNED: Sometimes you have to speak up to be heard.

24

New House, New School, New Friends

DAD'S BUSINESS was thriving. He spoke to his accountant if he could afford a bigger, more expensive house. The accountant confirmed that financially he could. We moved to South Eugene which was in a more expensive part of town. We were not rich but it was a bigger house in a nice neighborhood. That summer after sixth grade we moved into a two story white house with gray shutters. One of the most memorable aspects of that house is that it had a clothes shoot on the second floor where the clothes ended up in the laundromat on the first floor.

Our new house was far enough away that I did not see my friends from grade school at the new Junior High School. Most of my new friends were straight A students whose parents worked at the University of Oregon. For a while, I kept in contact with my friends from grade school but we were going in different directions. Eventually, I lost contact with my friends from grade school. The transition went well and I made new friends.

LESSONS LEARNED: Change can be good. Sometimes you have to let go of the past. New experiences can stretch you.

25

Playing Games as a Family

ALL THROUGH OUR GROWING UP YEARS we played many games together. We played card games such as Canasta and Hearts. Many an evening we would break out the card games. You learned strategy, competition and teamwork.

The outdoor games were football, basketball, and baseball. We had a basketball hoop on our house. Lots of the neighborhood kids came over to play. Since my mom baked cookies the kids would enjoy a delicious snack too. There was a park nearby where we played baseball with other kids in the area.

Remember, yard Jarts? They were large, lawn darts you threw into a ring. My brothers always stood way back when I threw my Jart. I was a wild Jart thrower. Who knows where it would land? I believe they are now outlawed. Lots of fun times playing together.

LESSON LEARNED: Do things together as a family which builds memories.

26

Confirmation

IN THE LUTHERAN CHURCH you went to confirmation classes for a couple of years and at the end you were confirmed. Confirmation is your foray into being a believer and adult in the church. We memorized Bible verses and studied the Bible. It was really rather boring. At the end before we were confirmed the Pastor asked each one of us if we believed in Jesus and thought we would go to heaven? All the other kids said "yes" but I did not. Pastor Lambert said to me "But Patty you grew up in the church." That was all he said. He never tried to talk to me later to find out more and help me understand faith. At that time, I didn't know if I believed in Jesus or not and I simply went to confirmation as a matter of rote and requirement. Again, the rigid, legalistic church that thought because you filled a church pew every weekend that it made you a believer. The Pastor still confirmed me but he never was genuinely concerned about my soul.

LESSONS LEARNED: Don't stay someplace because it is tradition. Sitting in a church pew every Sunday doesn't make you a believer. Sometimes you have to seek out your own faith.

27

Teen Years
TRYING TO FIT IN

MOST TEENS FEEL AWKWARD and they want to fit in. I was the same. By Junior High most of my girlfriends had boyfriends, but not me. I liked guys but never a boyfriend while I was in Junior High School. There was one very cute guy who had moved from California and his name was Rick. Rick had wavy, blonde hair and bright, blue eyes. He was so handsome. Since I didn't have a boyfriend then I started getting left out of invites to parties. Most of my girlfriends had boyfriends and they had their parties where only couples were invited. I felt left out. School dances were excruciating painful. None of the boys would ask me to dance. What is wrong with me? Am I not pretty enough? It was painful to watch the other teens dance while I stood on the sidelines. Usually, I would dance with my girlfriends.

Starting in 8th Grade, I permed my hair because I hated my straight hair. I felt like an "Ugly Duckling" and never pretty enough. Instead of being appreciative of my shiny, straight hair I always wanted to change it. My Mom and many of my friends had wavy hair therefore, I thought that was pretty. I wanted to fit in.

LESSONS LEARNED: Don't try to change yourself. Just do you. Fitting in is not always the answer.

28

Dad's Triple Artery Bypass

My Dad was in his mid 50s and seemed really healthy. He played volleyball on a weekly basis and he golfed. He had this perpetual pain in his chest. Finally, the doctor did an EKG and they found three of his arteries were blocked. This was a shock for our family. Dad had been a chain smoker most of his life. His doctor said it was a combination of smoking and stress which caused the blocked arteries. Dad had a triple artery bypass. We were all rather scared if Dad would make it through the surgery. Dad had always been a smoker but after the surgery he completely stopped smoking. We changed our diet and started eating healthier. Dad was only 56 years old when he had this surgery. It would be a foreshadowing of future heart problems for Dad. Yet, for many years, he led a healthy and active life.

LESSONS LEARNED: Never take anything for granted. Remember to love and appreciate your family and friends because one day they may be gone.

29

Disneyland

AFTER DAD'S SURGERY, he started living life differently. One of the ways was taking more vacations. Up to this time, we did road trips and traveled as cheaply as possible. Our vacations were road trips to Kansas and back. Not exactly a vacation with six people crammed into a station wagon! A highlight was going to Disneyland where we stayed in a beautiful hotel across the street from Disneyland. One of the rare times we stayed at a hotel instead of camping.

We woke up bright and early eagerly anticipating our day at Disneyland! We hopped on a ride called "It's a small world" with international dolls singing "It's a small world." I always loved dolls and seeing the brightly costumed dolls was the highlight of the trip. We tried out many great, ethnic restaurants. One Mexican food restaurant had food so hot it burned your lips.

This was the beginning of many fun vacations we did as a family.

LESSON LEARNED: Don't wait to live your life. Sometimes a life threatening event is a wakeup call to enjoy your life.

30

Creativity

FROM EARLY ON I enjoyed art, baking, and sewing. My mom was an excellent cook and seamstress. In school we had art classes. Starting at a young age, I baked cookies. Some type of creative element was in my life.

The smell of vanilla and sweet, smelling cookies during the holidays made for great memories. My Mom was a great cook and she taught me. She patiently showed me how to exactly measure out the ingredients and what order to mix everything together. We used recipes which were handed down from our grandma. Grandma was Norwegian therefore the food was rich and used ingredients like lard. Not very healthy for you but boy did it taste good. The recipes would say take a pinch of salt or a drop of food coloring. Later, I wrote the exact measurements down.

In 7th Grade I made holiday cookies which I shared with my classmates. Our teacher was a younger guy which all the girls swooned over but not me. I was not interested and he was our teacher, right? I remember happily talking with my classmates and sharing the cookies. The teacher wanted someone to come up to the front of the classroom to help him with a drawing for a gift. The other girls were raising their hands and screaming "me, me." I ignored the whole thing but surprisingly the teacher called on me to come up to the front of the class and help. I was shocked since I didn't think he even noticed me in his classroom. The reason, I remember this so well is that someone actually noticed me and made me feel valued. That did not happen very often to me.

One Christmas I decided to sew shirts for each of my brothers and I was in 8th Grade. For each of my brothers I made a different shirt for them. One shirt was western style with snap buttons and a collar. This was a complicated shirt to make.

For my other brother I sewed a polo shirt. And for my youngest brother a dress shirt. Loved making the shirts and giving them as gifts. This love for sewing went on for years. I even sewed myself a floral, suit jacket with matching skirt. Now, I think this is awful but back then I thought it was a beautiful suit.

LESSONS LEARNED: We all are creative. Learn to develop and enjoy the creative process.

31

High School

HIGH SCHOOL WAS A PRETTY QUIET TIME. I continued to be a good student and volunteered at school. Our school mascot was the "Axeman" since we were in Eugene where there were many trees. School colors were purple and white which they painted our gym these colors. It looked awful.

During high school, I took accounting and bookkeeping classes. I enjoyed the classes. In my Senior year, I was selected to handle the bookkeeping for the school. A group of us would spend the afternoon counting the cash till to make sure it balanced. Then, we completed balance sheets. Our accounting teacher oversaw the work. I enjoyed the volunteering and even thought for a split second that I would become an accountant. Nah! Still, it was great experience.

Finally, graduation day arrived. I graduated with honors and went through the graduation ceremony. In our family everyone assumed you would graduate from high school so this was not a big deal. We drove to the local Dairy Queen and I enjoyed a chocolate, mint ice cream. Still my favorite ice cream. That was the celebration. No big splashy parties. Parents didn't do huge parties in those days. The high school I attended you were expected to graduate.

LESSONS LEARNED: It is important to get your education. Focus and complete school with good grades.

32

My Cat Penny

MY VERY FIRST PET was Penny. He was a copper colored, long haired cat. A sweet cat. We found an ad for kittens and we went to choose a cat. Penny was a loving kitten and we brought him home. We thought the cat was female but when we took the cat to the Vet to get it fixed the Vet said he had news for us and that Penny was a male. As he grew, Penny's hinds legs became stiff and he had a hard time walking. My neighbor one time commented that Penny must be a "fighter" due to his constant limp. I explained that Penny had hip problems. One time, when I was on vacation for a few days when I returned home Mom said the cat hardly ate the whole time I was gone. This cat bonded with me and I bonded with him. He was my first pet. Penny was about two years old when his back legs froze up and he could not walk. Sadly, we had to let him go and put him down. One of the saddest days in my life. He was such a loving cat.

LESSONS LEARNED: Those that you love may not be in your life for very long but cherish the time that you have with them.

33

My Brother Jim

I HAVE AN OLDER BROTHER, JIM. He was also adopted from South Korea when he was four years old. Jim knew his biological family but they had given him up. When my Mom and Dad adopted Jim, he was one of the few minorities in our town. International adoptions were not common in those days. I asked my younger brother, Jon, why our parents catered to Jim? One possible reason was perhaps because our parents did not want to look like they were being prejudiced. Jim had no rules that applied to him unlike the rest of us who had to follow our parent's rules. He could be late or stay out as late as he wanted too. Dad did not hold Jim accountable for anything therefore, Jim felt entitled.

My Dad always gave him everything on a silver platter and treated Jim like he was the oldest child. Even though we had our oldest brother, Paul, who was actually my parent's biological child. Jim did everything right in my Dad's eyes. He was athletic, handsome and smart. But Jim had an annoying habit of being late all the time. For my parent's 25th Wedding Anniversary we bought an engraved plate for them. Jim was the one picking up the plate from the engraver and he was bringing it to the Anniversary celebration. Again, he was late for dinner and we all had to wait for him since he had the gift. We were exasperated at how rude Jim was for holding up the whole Anniversary celebration. It did not phase Jim a bit. Later on when our Mom died, Jim didn't even go to her funeral. The ultimate act of being ungrateful. Jim was mad at our Mom at the time and he didn't want to fly to attend her funeral. Unfortunately, Jim is the "Black sheep" in our family. I have forgiven Jim but we realize he has to live with himself. Also, Jim was so angry every time we talked to him and everyone had done him wrong. It is sad when someone you love and your family member is not happy.

LESSONS LEARNED: Your kids need guidelines to help them build good character. Forgive even if the person doesn't deserve it.

34

Dad Gets Bubonic Plague

MY DAD, WHO NEVER GOT SICK, came down with a fever and sweating. Finally, after a couple days of this he went to his doctor. The doctor immediately had him taken to the hospital and quarantined. Because it is a highly infectious disease, we could only see him if we were fully suited up with body covering and masks. Dad was there for a week. They guessed that he got the disease from our mountain property. Likely a flea had jumped off a rodent onto our dog and then onto Dad. Dad recovered but it was pretty scary.

LESSONS LEARNED: Life can change in a blink of an eye. Be grateful for your health.

35

First Microwave

MOM AND I WENT TO A COOKING CLASS to learn how to use the microwave oven. Microwave ovens had recently come out on the market and we were curious. I still remember we made cream of broccoli soup. We watched in amazement how food can be made in only a few minutes. This was truly a miracle. Making the soup was so quick and easy. Another technology that revolutionized our lives. Before it took a long time to heat up food but now you could heat food up in a minute. Microwave dinners were being made. We were so astounded how much faster you could get things done. When we returned home and shared with Dad about this miraculous cooking technology, he promptly bought one for us. This was also the beginning of the "microwave world" we live in where we want everything now. Our lives started to reflect that microwave mentality of hurry up and no patience needed. It needs to be done quickly and now.

LESSONS LEARNED: Sometimes the fastest way isn't the best way. With rushing things there comes a price. In our society the price is demanding everything is done in minutes and no patience for waiting. Slow cooking and slowing down in life has its advantages.

36

Working for Dad

HIGH SCHOOL GRADUATION DAY ended. The next day was a workday and I started working with my Dad. He was a State Farm insurance agent he had his own agency in Eugene. My whole life we had planned on my working for Dad. It was a given. Dad had built up a successful insurance agency. I still lived at home with Mom and Dad. Dad would drive us to and from work each day. In the beginning, it was ideal because I had work and he had a reliable employee. After all, I lived with Dad and then likely I wouldn't quit. I enjoyed talking with people and learning. I was good at sales and learned quickly. Dad became one of the top earning agents while I worked with him.

During this time, I learned a lot about the business world and how to interact with customers. There was so much to learn about insurance. In those days, we did not have computers and the quotes were all manually done with a pen and paper. We had a rate manual that gave us the rating factors based on specifics about the driver.

After working for a couple years with Dad, I suggested we offer increasing the auto liability limits for our clients by sending them a quote for the price difference if they increased those limits. I would calculate and mail out a quote to each customer who had low liability limits. My Dad had the highest average auto premiums of any of the agents in his group of agents. He was happy with this recognition and it was a good service to the clients.

My Dad became friends with many of his clients. We would go out to their homes and visit the families. One time they let us pick the left over filberts from their orchard. Dad taught me that clients need not be an impersonal interaction, but can become friends too.

Dad worked very hard and hardly ever took a vacation. He would often do evening appointments. He listed our home phone number in the Yellow Pages and usually received calls at home. We learned to handle calls from customers even early on. Service was always important to Dad and especially being available for emergency calls.

Computers were becoming more popular and we finally got computers at the office. It forever changed how we did business. Instead of manually calculating the rates the computer did the calculations. Actually, Dad was a fast learner and he really loved the computers.

When we first got computers in my Dad's office, little did I know how that would revolutionize the world. Yes, I am old. I did not grow up with computers. The first computers I learned on were State Farm computers in the agent's office. After a couple of years working in the insurance office they started using computers. This was amazing. All the customers information was on the computer instead of only a paper file. We still kept paper files but it was convenient to look up their information and not move from your desk. Calculating the insurance rates was so much easier too. Using the computer for calculating rates was so much faster and accurate. This was the start of the computer era.

Oh my, it was a long six years! Living with your parents and working with a parent is challenging. I am sure it was challenging for Dad too. My Dad was a perfectionist and everything had to be just right. We fought often. The fights would continue at home too. My poor Mom! This was to set a pattern for guys I would date or marry in the future: controlling men.

LESSONS LEARNED: Don't stay in a job forever if it is crushing your soul. Parents are human too. Learn from the difficult times too.

37

First Boyfriend, First Broken Heart

A LOCAL PHOTOGRAPHY GROUP met once a month in a meeting room in Eugene. We shared our photos with one another and received critiques on how to improve. There were local field trips taking scenic and portrait shots. Growing creatively and learning a new skill was a highlight of my life during this time. When I was 20 years old, I met my first boyfriend, Don, through this photography club. He had wavy, brown hair and green eyes. He was a craftsman and outdoorsy guy. For Valentines he gave me the biggest Valentine card I have ever received. So sweet.

We had been dating a few months and I invited Don to my parent's house for Thanksgiving dinner. It seemed like a good idea at the time. My Dad did not say one word to Don. Dad normally was a very social person and he never met a stranger. Not in this case. Sometimes "Father does know best."

For several months we dated and things seemed to be going well. Then, one day he called me and broke up with me. I was crushed. I cried and cried and cried.

My poor Mom did not know what to do. It would be years before I dated again.

Looking back now, I realized the relationship could not last in the long run. Don was a great guy but our lives were going in different directions.

LESSONS LEARNED: First loves can be crushing when they end but life goes on. Maybe, your parents do know what is best for you.

38

Getting my Driver's License

I have always been a late bloomer and I was 20 years old before I got my driver's license. Before then, I had no interest in driving. It only took me three times to pass my driving test. The test was so stressful that I would mess up but I finally passed. All of my other brothers were anxious to get their license as soon as they could. My first car was a Chevrolet Chevette. To this day, I called it the "shove it" because it was such a crap piece of car. Now that I could drive it gave me a new freedom. I didn't have to rely on others to drive me everywhere. Freedom!

LESSONS LEARNED: Do something even if it is difficult to have more independence. Don't depend on someone else for everything.

39

My First Solo Vacation

I WAS 20 YEARS OLD and I wasn't doing anything besides working and going home. Then the idea of taking a vacation by myself took hold. I booked with a group tour up through Washington state and Canada. This vacation was the beginning of many changes in my life and a catalyst.

Early one morning, I excitedly flew from Portland to Seattle. I joined the group at the busy airport where we boarded a luxury bus. Since, I did not know any other travelers, I took my chances and let the tour company choose my roommate for me. I was paired with a 70 year old lady from Galveston, Texas named Ruth. She was hilarious. One time she was laundering her underwear and placed it on the railing outside our room. A gust of wind picked up the underwear as it floated down to the street. We both had a good laugh. She was a great roommate.

We wound through heavily forested roads and glimpsed the majestic Mount Rainier. Our first major stop was the Hoh rain forest in Washington which had the most rainfall of anywhere in the USA. Thick moss hung from every tree. Walking through the forest a light mist permeated the air. We went back to the lodge and we smelled the heavenly salmon on the grill. The next leg of our trip was going to Vancouver, British Columbia. We boarded a large ferry and as we entered the harbor the elegant Empress hotel appeared at the end of the harbor. We drove to the beautiful, Butchart Gardens which were brightly colored gardens and carefully, manicured. Rows and rows of every imaginable flower flourished there. There were themes at the garden. One was an English garden and another was a Japanese garden. At night they had a light show which was spectacular.

On this trip, we went up to the Bugaboo Mountains in British Columbia. They parked the bus and small groups of us were transported by helicopter to the lodge. You could only get to the place by helicopter. This is the first and only time I would be in a helicopter. I did not know what to expect but seeing the view from the helicopter was a thrill. Every morning, we started our day with a breakfast made from scratch by the chef. Then we would go by helicopter up into the Bugaboos and hike around all day in the pristine snow. Spectacular, jagged mountains and bright, blue skies were our view each day. We would take a break for lunch where they would fly in our delicious lunch. And they didn't feed us stale bread and lunch meat. This was gourmet. By early evening we all were transported back to the lodge where we started with enjoying a glass of wine. Our dinners were family style and again every meal was a gourmet masterpiece. One of the most memorable trips I have ever taken.

Getting away from the normal routine was life changing. This trip was a catalyst in my life. During this vacation, I decided that I needed to move into my own apartment, go to a different church, and find a different job. My eyes opened to the possibilities in my life. Up to this point, I had felt stuck. Simply being away for a few days made me realize there is a whole world out there. As soon as I returned home, I shared with my parents that I was moving out of their house. My parents were not very happy. You would think they would love to get their kids out of the house. My parents would be happy if we all lived with them or a next door to them for the rest of our lives. My Dad did not have a stable upbringing therefore, having a close family was very important to him. Anytime, one of us kids would want to be more independent it was stressful for Dad.

LESSONS LEARNED: Get outside of a situation to get a clearer perspective. Sometimes being in a different place will be a catalyst. You can get unstuck

40
New Church

MY WHOLE LIFE I had been raised in a very rigid, legalistic, Lutheran church. It was stand up, sit down, shut up and repeat after us. I felt like if I didn't find a different church then I would leave the church altogether. But first I wanted to find a place which gave me joy and grew my faith. I started looking around and found another Lutheran church where I felt uplifted and the folks were friendly. The music was upbeat and the sermons applied to our lives.

One day while at the gym working out I met a gal named Janice. We hit it off and became friends. Janice was a Christian too and we had that in common. Both of us were single and looking for more fellowship with other Christians. We met with a few friends and we started a Christian, singles group. The word got out through the other churches in the area and we had gatherings with 20-30 people. The core group planned events such as hiking, potlucks and worship. I realized life did not have to be so serious especially in church or with other Christians. A whole world of new friends opened up to me and I enjoyed planning events.

LESSONS LEARNED: Don't stay with a religious organization just because you grew up there. Church can be fun and uplifting.

41

Born Again

I NOTICED THE OTHER CHRISTIANS were joyful and were excited about their faith. I did not have that. What was wrong with my faith?

Then, I had a bad car accident and I totaled my car. It was completely my fault and I felt so much guilt over the accident. Fortunately, no one was hurt but my car was wrecked. For two weeks, I didn't go anywhere but work and home. My Dad would drive me to work and home again. One day, my Dad could see that I was depressed. He recommended that I go and see my Christian friends and he would drove me there. I still remember a friend who said to me "Jesus loves you." and I broke down with a torrent of tears. My life was changed and I felt a huge heaviness lift from me. A load had been lifted. Religion was not merely traditions and repeating what someone else said. I realized in my life even if I did something wrong that I was not a bad person. God had taken all of that guilt away through Jesus Christ sacrifice for all of us. My life had meaning and I am precious in God's sight. Also, that God had my life in His hands.

LESSONS LEARNED: Even when you mess up God still loves you. Faith is not a building or rituals but what is in your heart.

42

Vacation in Hawaii

I LOVED PHOTOGRAPHY and I found a group tour going to Hawaii and led by a professional photographer. We went to the gorgeous island of Maui. We all piled into a van and headed out on the narrow, winding road to Hana. We looked out the window at deep ravines off the side of the road. Exhilarating and scary as hell. This was one of the most amazing vacations I have taken. The trip allowed me to explore my creative side in a gorgeous setting.

Also, vacations away from the family was one more way of exerting my independence from Mom and Dad. I had been sheltered most of my life and did almost everything with my parents growing up.

One funny story is a few of us went to the "red beach" to take photos. As we came around the corner, we found out it was a nudist beach! Here we had our cameras with telephoto lenses. In embarrassment, we all turned around and back the way we came.

In the evenings we made meals family style making dinner at our condo. During the day, we shopped at the fruit stands along the road. Food was pretty expensive in Hawaii but we still had delicious meals.

LESSONS LEARNED: Explore and have adventures in life. Go outside of the norm.

43
College

FINALLY, I had the guts to move on and enroll in college. This was very challenging because Dad would have loved it if I worked for him the rest of my life. I loved my Dad but it was time to move on. Gave my Dad a one year notice to hire someone to replace me at his office. Then, I went to a private college, in Portland, Oregon called Concordia University and I obtained a degree in education.

We drove to a small, campus with tall trees. The buildings were red brick and looked historic. This college only had 500 students. We went to the all-girls dorm where I would live for the first year of college. I put my luggage on a twin, bunk bed in a sparse room with cold floors. My roommate was a 17 year old girl from Hermiston, Oregon. For a split second, I wondered what I was doing going to college at 24 years of age. Most of the other students were recent high school graduates.

Since, this was a private, Christian college we had worship every morning and several evenings a week. I loved it that I started my day off singing hymns and gathering with other believers. Then, in the evening the students led the worship and Bible study time. My girlfriend, Robin, and I usually led the evening worship.

This made us dig into the Bible and grow in our faith. One of the advantages of attending a small college is that you can be more involved in the activities at the college.

One memorable experience was when I had to sing solo in front of my peers as a final project for taking singing lessons. I always loved singing but my brothers would tell me not to sing too loudly in church since I sang off key. When they offered private singing lessons I jumped on the chance to improve my singing. Little did I know that I would have to sing in front of my classmates. This was a very small college that I attended therefore, I knew about everyone. In addition, I was still petrified of speaking in public. I made it through the recital but I was terrified anyway. This was a milestone for me to do something which I was terrible at and still doing it. Glad I did it but at the time I was very nervous.

One of my lifelong loves, which is making cards, began when I was in college. The whole card making and scrap booking craze was becoming popular then. The bookstore managers taught a card making class and I was hooked. I loved the process, technique and outcome. Ever since then I have made cards for over 30 years. Later, the two ladies opened a scrap-booking store in Portland, Oregon.

In my third year of college, I was a dorm director at the college I attended. The positive side is that my room and board was paid for. The downside is that I hardly slept that year. It was like having 40 kids you needed to watch over. Since this was a private college no alcohol was allowed on premises. In addition, the dorms had to be cleared out except for the residences at midnight each night. Therefore, every night at midnight I would walk the hallways and scooting the non-residents out of the dorm. Usually, these were girlfriends. I supervised a dorm of with all guys. Not my idea but my boss thought it would be a good idea. The only year they had the dorm director who was female (me) supervise a dorm of men. It was quite the experience.

What happened is that most of the guys did not communicate with me. Several of the residences were from other countries such as Hong Kong or Japan. One sunny afternoon I walked by the room of one of the guys then I asked them if everything was okay. They said they were fine but I sensed something was wrong. A few minutes later one of the guys came to my dorm apartment and said they broke their tooth. I drove them to a dentist.

During the summer most of the students left for the summer. One student who lived in Japan went back home for the summer. He had bought a baby rabbit and he asked me to take care of the rabbit for him. I agreed thinking how hard can this be? This was a cute, lop eared rabbit. I fed the rabbit carrots every day because rabbits love carrots, right? After a few days of this diet the rabbit refused to eat anymore carrots! One day I decided to get a collar and leash for the rabbit to "walk" him outside. Have you ever heard a rabbit scream? It was a terrible sound and sounded like a child screaming. The walks were cut short. Then for a week, I went to visit my parents in Eugene and left the rabbit with my girlfriend. I had instructed her how to feed and water the rabbit. After the week, I came back and obviously one of its long ears had gangrene and half of the ear was dead. I took the rabbit to a vet who said the ear had to be cut off where the gangrene infected the ear. That was an $80 bill which I paid. This rabbit was getting expensive. During that summer, I had decided to rent a room in a house. The retired couple were good to the rabbit and fed it a variety of garden food. One day

I returned home when my landlord said the rabbit had broken free of the cage and ran away. My first thought is "Yes!" the rabbit is gone and I don't have to take care of it anymore. A couple of days pass and I come home. My landlord informed me that guess what, the rabbit had returned. Damn! The rabbit's owner returned to college. I gave him back his rabbit which had half of an ear chopped off and the $80 vet bill. He gave me this look of what the hell happened to his cute rabbit but he didn't say anything. He took his rabbit and reimbursed me. Whew! No more bunny!

One evening, we were winding along the coast in the car my girlfriend was driving. She was going very fast along the narrow coastal road which was raining heavily. We could hardly see and it was pitch black. I remember Kimberlee saying she is a "thrill seeker" and about that time she lost control of the car. The car slid off the road towards the ocean. Everything went into slow motion. You know how you have those moments when life suddenly goes surreal like you are in a dream and you think your life is flashing before your eyes? I felt that way and I could see us slowly going off the road towards the cliff. I sent up a prayer and thought this is it, we bit the dust. All of a sudden, the car stopped. I scrambled out of the car since friends were following us in their car. I went up to the road to flag them down. They helped Kimberlee get out of her car and we called a tow truck. The truck pulled the car out of the cliff. What was so shocking is that nothing was damaged on the car, not even the front grill. Even more amazing is that neither one of us were hurt. We didn't have a bruise or scratch on us. I truly believe that angels stopped us from hurtling all the way down to the ocean. It was not my time yet. God still had a plan and purpose for my life. Scariest day of my life so far!

LESSONS LEARNED: Sometimes folks don't want you to fly out of the nest but make the leap anyway. Flying out of the nest is actually freeing. Waiting for everyone's approval stagnates your life.

44

Make-Up Counters

MOM WAS A "TOMBOY" so she wore very little make-up and had not taught me how to wear make-up. In my late teens, I went to the make-up counters at department stores to learn this art of make-up application. I always loved girly things and make up was one of those things I loved too. Most of the folks had no idea how to apply make up for Asian eyes. Usually, I would walk out of the store looking like a clown with bright blue eye shadow up to my eyebrows. It was hideous. After many years, I finally learned how to apply make-up which looked better on an Asian face.

LESSONS LEARNED: Beauty is not what social media tells you but what is within. You don't have to look the same as everyone else. Value your own uniqueness.

45

Teaching 8th Graders, Heaven Or Hell?

MY WHOLE LIFE I wanted to be a teacher. I loved helping people and I enjoyed reading. This is why I chose a degree in Language Arts. After college graduation I started applying at various school districts. The Principal at a middle school interviewed me to teach 8th graders at an inner city, school in Portland, Oregon. To my shock and excitement I was hired.

The first day of school I arrived early excited to start the day. There were 30 students staring back at me. Rather intimidating. We started the morning with introductions and a simple lesson plan. At first, I was excited to share and teach the kids. In my classroom about 60% of the students were nonwhite. They were African American, Asian, Russian, Vietnamese and Hispanic. Up to this point, I had been mostly around whites. During this time, I learned a lot about many cultures and family situations. Some parents were very involved in their kid's life. Other times, the parents were nowhere to be found. Sad.

Each of my classes had at least 30 students with no help. Almost, on a daily basis the kids would swear at me. Basically, every day I received verbal abuse from the students. About once a month there was a fist fight in my own classroom. Every Sunday evening I would cry before going to sleep. This was not how I thought teaching would turn out.

When the students learned and the light bulb turned on was a highlight of teaching. One of those "Aha" times was when I taught a poetry lesson. This lesson went over various types of poetry and we added artwork too. We had fun. The students grew their creative skills. At the end of the lesson, a tall, gangly student shared with me saying "Mrs. Brenner, I thought poetry was going to be boring but you made it fun." One comment from a student who loved learning was the reward for teaching. He enjoyed learning and he realized school doesn't have to be boring. The light bulb moment of why teaching is worthwhile.

One of my students had recently moved from Vietnam. Every day she would stay after school and help me clean up the classroom. I rewarded her with a can of soda. She had never had soda before and her face puckered up. Here I was thinking that I was rewarding her with a great treat. So funny because other kids would love a can of pop. Since she hadn't grown up with it the taste was not something she was used too. Many times I went over to her family's house and had dinner with them. She was a sweet person.

One of the most memorable and stressful situations was when the students went into a mutiny one day. All the kids had assigned seating. One morning as I gave them their new assigned seating all the kids started banging on their desks and said, "no more assigned seating." This was led by a girl in the classroom who was a gang leader. She was a force and everyone followed her lead. I had no idea what to do. They never taught me how to handle a mutiny when I was in student teaching. I went out into the hallway and looked for someone to help me. The Vice Principal broke up the ruckus. After having a cry then I met with my Master teacher on how to handle this situation. She said single out the ring leaders then have each one of the ring leaders sent to separate classrooms. The remaining kids would be made to work on their lessons and not given any free time during the class time. This worked.

The students were arriving for our Home Room class. Suddenly, one of my female students started whaling on a boy. I was in shock. I don't know what was going on but apparently she was pretty pissed at him. I would never put myself between students when they were fighting. My Vice Principle broke up the fight. Crazy

For several months the students in my class were Pen Pals with kids from another school. They enjoyed writing to each other. We planned a field trip to the Zoo. They wanted to meet in person therefore, we planned the event. There were over 100 students who went on the trip. We organized volunteers, bus, food, and a scavenger hunt. The kids had a blast. One of my first experiences of planning a group event. We didn't lose any kids, no fights, and we had fun. Successful event!

I taught for four years. Eventually, I got better at teaching. It was one of the hardest jobs and best jobs I ever had. Not because I had fun but because it built character in me. Growing up my life had been cushy. Seeing kids from all walks of life was life-changing.

Eventually, I was so stressed with teaching that I knew that I had to leave.

LESSONS LEARNED: Sometimes your toughest job can be your best job. Even though it was the most stressful job I have ever had it stretched me as a person. Plus, I learned about many different cultures. As the saying goes "What doesn't kill you makes you stronger."

46
Terry

I WAS SINGLE and wanted to meet other singles. There was a group called Bergfreunde which was a group for singles. They had lots of activities and was a fun group.

They had outdoor volleyball at a park in Portland, Oregon. During this time, I met Terry playing volleyball. The first thing he said to me is "you have Spanish skin and Asian eyes, what are you?" Should have been a sign that he asked me this since I had been asked my whole life, What are you? Anyway, it struck up a conversation and I talked to him. He said he was a Christian and which was important to me. Terry already had three kids from a prior marriage. He seemed sweet and we had fun together. We liked to go to garage sales. We played volleyball and went hiking.

Terry worked as a Real Estate agent. Or rather he didn't work, therefore, I paid his rent at his apartment. This should have been a "sign" to me.

LESSONS LEARNED: Don't pay for a boyfriend or girlfriend's rent. Be aware of "red flags" that the person is a leach and going to take advantage of you.

47
Dad Dies

ON MOTHER'S DAY, I got a call from my family that Dad has gone into a coma. He was at home and he was rushed to the hospital which was a distance from their home. We stayed at hospital day and night for several days. Finally, after a week Dad passed on. It was the longest week of my life. I was in the hospital room with Mom and I distinctly remember seeing Dad turn his head and look at mom when he died. The whole time he was in the coma, he never opened his eyes or moved his head. It was like he wanted to look one last time at Mom. If you don't believe someone has a "spirit" in them then be around them when they die. Dad didn't even look the same and all color left his face.

I went into shock. It was all so sudden and I had seen Dad the week before. There was a mix of grief and guilt. I realized that I had never been fully grateful or expressed to Dad how much I loved him. The grief lingered for years. Say what you need to your loved ones while you can.

Going back to work, I was a zombie. One of my sweet students brought me flowers. The kids who were normally noisy were so quiet the first day I returned to teaching. They felt my grief and had respect for my loss.

My Dad was only in his sixties when he passed away. I felt like an orphan again. My mom went into a depression. Then I felt the double whammy of feeling like I lost both of my parents, even though my Mom was still alive. She wasn't there for me emotionally. I felt so abandoned again.

LESSONS LEARNED: Life can change drastically and suddenly. Make sure that you tell you loved ones that you love them. Recognize the grieving process.

48

Marriage—Love Or Not?

AT THIS TIME, I was still dating Terry. We had not talked about marriage. One day Terry tells me that his Dad asked when we were going to get married. I said that is a "sign" and let's do it. No romantic proposal from Terry. No ring in hand. Again, this should have been a "sign." I was still grieving so much and getting married seemed like it was the thing to do. Also, I was in my early thirties and felt like I was getting too old to not be married.

We asked my Mom for her blessing on the marriage. She said only God gives Blessings. Maybe it was her way of not approving of the marriage. Mom was not very assertive so she would not tell me what to do.

Our wedding ceremony was a small one at a quaint church in Portland. After wards, the reception was at a friend's house. Then we flew to Hawaii for our honeymoon.

At the beginning our marriage seemed to be good. Yet, I was blind to the signs of Terry's control and beginning of his abuse. A big red flag was on the honeymoon in Hawaii was when Terry wanted to stay at the beach all day long. Then, it would be over 12 hours between meals because he didn't want to stop to eat. I had bought the wedding rings, paid for the wedding and honeymoon. All of these things should have been a warning "sign." I was so naive. The beginning of 11 years of stress and turmoil.

LESSONS LEARNED: Make sure that you are treated with respect. Others treat you as you allow them to treat you. If you are doing all the giving then this is a sure sign of an unhealthy relationship.

49

Selling On eBay

ONLINE SELLING was in the early years. A company called eBay started a platform where anyone could sell to anyone in the world. For almost 15 years, I sold on eBay. Since we both enjoyed going to garage sales and thrifting it was an outlet to make additional income. I did it on top of a full time job. Terry and I would go out to garage sales early in the morning and scope out our finds. I was good at finding "treasures." Then, I would clean up the item, take photos and list on eBay in the evenings and weekends. I learned how to work with customers, what customers wanted and about having my own business. In the early days of eBay about everything we listed sold right away. It was when eBay was new and people were excited to buy online.

There were not any other online selling platforms like eBay. Overall, I enjoyed doing this because I liked the thrill of the "hunt" snagging my "prize" and being rewarded. The drawback was that I did this on top of working full time, cooking, and cleaning. Terry was such a perfectionist and many times it was around midnight and I was still editing and correcting the eBay listing the way Terry wanted it. Then, I would have to be at work at 7 am the next morning. I asked him one time why doesn't he learn how to do this? He said he didn't want to learn. Why would he need to learn since he had me doing it all!? During our marriage Terry would get us into many extra side businesses. I usually worked a full time job on top of a part time job with Terry.

LESSONS LEARNED: Learning new skills is good. Being your own boss can be fun. Sometimes, cutting edge tools, such as eBay, can explode. Don't let others use you.

50

New Name

ALL THROUGH GRADE SCHOOL I went by Patty. My formal name is Patricia. My brothers and kids in school would make fun of me and say, "fatty Patty" and other words that rhymed with Patty. Believe me there are a lot of mean words that rhyme with Patty.

Then later in my teens I started going by Pat. I felt like it sounded more grown up and not so childish. Yet, the sound of the name felt harsh and not very girly. Neither name seemed to fit me. In my late 20's, I decided to change my name. At first, I liked the name Kim but it had no association with any part of my name. I mentioned this to my Mom and she said everyone in Korea is named Kim. True that Kim is a very common last name in Korea. Then, I started going by my middle name of "Ann." It felt softer and more feminine. The meaning of the name Ann is grace or "God has favored me." This meaning fits. I do feel that my life has favor.

LESSONS LEARNED: Go ahead and risk making changes. You are not going to die. For many years, Staying with what makes other people happy is not the reason to not make a change. Changing your name is huge because your name is part of your identity.

51

New Career at State Farm
SQUARE PEG IN ROUND HOLE

CONTINUING IN TEACHING was becoming too stressful. I needed to look for another job. My Dad was an agent for State Farm Insurance and they had a good reputation. I was looking for a stable job with good pay and benefits. I drove down to Salem from Portland. It had snowed than morning which is rare for Oregon. When I arrived at the office all the lights were off and no one was there except for the interviewer. Asked him why no one else was there and he said it was a snow day so they closed the office. He said he still came to the office to see who would show up for the interview. Well, I showed up. I went through the interview process and low and behold they hired me. Only 3% of the applicants who apply for a job at State Farm get hired.

Dress code was still wearing suits so I went out and bought three suits from Petite Sophisticate. These three suits rotated in my wardrobe for years.

First day of work, I was so excited and giddy. I could not believe my good fortune. Landed a great job with a great company. I was working as an Auto Underwriter. You assess the risk of the policyholder to ensure that they are a profitable policy. It was tightrope between keeping your agents happy and your boss happy.

We sat in cubicles in rows with co-workers only inches from one another. My co-worker was supposed to be my assistant but she would make faces at me when no one was looking. For some reason, she did not like me and made my time there difficult. Also, State Farm is very corporate. You had to follow the corporate policies which no one explained to you. By learning you figured out what they expected.

At a particularly negative staff meeting I spoke up and said why are we so scared of saying what we really think? Not a response from anyone but dead silence. Everyone had to agree with our boss or you were the problem. My Supervisor said how embarrassed she was by my outburst and this was inappropriate. She told me I was wrong for speak up in the meeting. The management wanted "yes men" and no real individuality. I realized it was a toxic environment and I needed to get out soon.

One of the good points of working for State Farm was that I could volunteer outside of the office. I enjoyed helping build a house for Habitat for Humanity. During this time, I taught continuing education courses to insurance agents. I volunteered at the local schools. Plus, the good income allowed me to take fantastic vacations to Hawaii and beautiful places.

LESSONS LEARNED: Do not try to fit into a job which squashes you. Also, even if it is not the ideal job you learn from every situation good or bad.

52

Back to the Motherland
FINDING MY ROOTS

I WAS CONSIDERING ADOPTING A CHILD from South Korea therefore, I wanted to learn more about the culture. I was almost 40 years old. This was my first trip back to Korea after leaving there at age four. Holt Adoption Agency offered a "Motherland Tour" for any adoptees who were born in Korea and later adopted. Our trip started at the Seattle airport where there were around 40 of us. They took a group photo of us in our American dress. Later, they would take a photo of us in Korean dress. This was the beginning of learning more about myself and the cultural heritage which are my roots.

The jet we boarded was huge and had two stories. It was a long plane ride to Korea but comfortable. All of the airline stewardesses looked like clones of each other. Same height, body type and facial features. And of course, they all looked like models. Kind of weird but maybe that was how it was with Koreans. A standardized idea of beauty.

We traveled all over South Korea and saw old palaces, gardens and the country. We visited the regular tourist spots. Our first leg of the trip was staying at the older but clean orphanage in Seoul. When, we arrived we could smell rice cooking and the distinct smell of Kim chi. During our stay at the orphanage we had 40 people sharing two showers. I was up by 4 am every morning so I could take a shower before the others woke up. We ate Korean food every day and had Kim Chi morning, noon and night. We started smelling like Kim chi. Good thing that I loved Kim chi. We slept on the floor on mats in true Korean culture. Some of the others complained but I didn't care. Before the trip, I thought I would not enjoy staying at the orphanage but it was a blast. All of us girls slept together in one room and it was a week-long slumber party. We stayed up late and talked about life and dreams.

The highlight of that trip was going to the unwed mother's home. This was heart rending knowing the moms would have to give up their babies. Visiting the home gave us insight into our own adoption. The mothers stayed here until their babies were born and then gave their baby up for adoption. Many of the mothers knew the sex of their baby without taking tests. A mom's instinct is strong. A mother shared with us how happy she was to meet us and to see that we have good lives. Brought a lump to our throats and brought tears to my eyes. Even though they knew they would likely never see their child again they were appreciative to know the babies went to loving families.

Another special part of the trip was visiting the orphanages. Kids who have disabilities usually do not get adopted. While it was sad they would never have their own family the kids were lovingly treated at the orphanage. The kids were in classes for music, writing, math and art. Many of these kids were artistic. It made my heart feel good knowing they always had a place to live.

At one point, our tour guide, David Kim, said to me that during the time I was in the orphanage that many of the babies died. It stabbed my heart to think of the many fragile babies who never made it. Also, I felt very grateful that I survived. I have always been a survivor and a fighter. Realizing that God had a plan and a purpose for my life.

A gorgeous part of our trip was going to Cheju Island or the Hawaii of Korea. We flew there from the mainland and saw pristine, white sandy beaches. Modern, luxury hotels reached to the sky against a brilliant, blue sky. Such a relaxing and lovely place.

We visited the world's largest Christian church which had one million members. This place was like a huge football field it was so big. The sermon was interpreted in several different languages. They even introduced our group over the loudspeaker which made us feel special.

A memorable part of our trip was the custom made Hanbok or Korean dress. We chose the colors and I chose pink and lavender. The tailor measured us so the Hanbok fit perfectly. There was a group photo taken and we looked so different from the first group photo when we were wearing our American clothing.

One night we stayed with a Host family. They fed us delicious, aromatic food until we could not squeeze in one more bite. The next morning as we were ready to leave the host mom had big tears streaming down her face. I was so touched.

This was the first time I had been around so many Korean adoptees at the same time. Many adoptees had loving families and a good life. Unfortunately, some were raised in abusive families or had very low self-esteem. I realized that I had been raised in a loving home.

LESSONS LEARNED: Learning about your cultural heritage gives you more insight into the culture you came from and what influences you as a person. Be proud of your heritage. Even though I was raised by German American parents, I gravitated towards all things Asian. I loved Asian food and design.

53

Colorado
NEW JOB, NEW HOME

STATE FARM HAD OPENED UP a new regional office in Greeley, Colorado. Anyone in the country from anywhere could apply for those jobs. I applied but really thought I had a slim chance of getting a job there. After all this was open to everyone who worked with State Farm countrywide to apply. To my shock they wanted to fly me out for an interview.

Several of us took a plane from Portland to Denver for the interviews. Driving from Denver to Windsor I took Highway 85. Two things struck me, how brown the landscape looked and the magnificent Rocky Mountains. Since it was the Greeley Stampede week the only hotels available were in Windsor.

I found the hotel and checked in. That evening I roamed to a local restaurant in Windsor. A little boy that was with his family at a nearby table loudly asked his parents while pointing at me if that woman is Japanese? After finishing dinner, I was waiting for the waitress to take my money. Sat there and sat there. The waitress was at another table folding napkins. She could see me but didn't come over to my table. Finally, the cook came out from the kitchen and asked if I needed anything. I said I was ready to pay my bill. I don't know if the waitress was not paying attention or purposely ignoring me. I chalked it up to that she didn't realize I was ready to pay my bill and I didn't think anymore of the incident. Then later that day, I went to the grocery store in Windsor. When shopping several people stared at me like I was an alien from another planet. I had already lived in different cities in the Northwest and traveled but never that this reaction to me. With the combination of situations I finally guessed that due to being nonwhite folks were treating me differently. I vowed right then that I would never live in Windsor. At that time Windsor was more closed off and not so mixed with folks from various places.

I had applied for a lateral job position as an Underwriter. In the interview with the Life Division Superintendents they asked me if I would take a job as a supervisor in that department? I said that I felt like I needed to be knowledgeable in that department first. I didn't say no to that job. They offered me a job as a Supervisor job in the Life Insurance division. I was shocked. The doors opened. Not only did I get the job but a job which was one step above the job I had applied for initially. It was meant to be for me to move to Colorado and get that job. Someone bigger than me had His hand in this.

I supervised 20 people who worked in the mail room. Since we had just opened the office most of the workers were temporary staff. One day I went into the mail room and two women were on the floor fighting and tearing each other's hair out. I immediately sent them home and told the staffing agency to not send them back again. Not what I was expecting when supervising at a corporate company!

Another one of my employees shared with me that she was pregnant with twins and they were not by her husband but a married man. Wow, who would know it was going to be such a Peyton Place!

Then another employee had his mom call me to say he was a "good boy." He had not shown up for work for three days and no call from him. Later, I found out he had received a DUI ticket and he was sitting in jail. Crazy!

On the other hand, we had a wonderful division manager who wanted to be inclusive and bring fun to the workplace. Her name was Sandy. Sandy was half Korean and half white. Her mom was Korean who met her Dad in Korea. At age six, Sandy's family moved from Korea to America to give Sandy a better life. In Korea if you are mixed race you were not accepted in that culture. Sandy grew up in America and had a great career with State Farm. She was the manager of the Life Insurance division with State Farm. Another American success story. I admired Sandy.

Terry and I moved out to Colorado and lived in Greeley. Everything was exciting. New boss new job and new place. Life was perfect.

LESSONS LEARNED: Grab for the "golden ring" and you might just win. Logically, I should never have been hired for this job which was at a higher job level. If the doors are meant to open then they will. Have more belief in yourself.

54

Divorce

OVER TIME, Terry was very verbally abusive. I could do nothing right. Everything I did he controlled, even how long I could talk to my family on the phone. Near the end of our marriage, Terry would get so mad that he had his fist only inches from my face threatening to punch me. Almost every day, he would call me up at work about every day to swear at me about something he thought that I did wrong. Then, I would come home and it was more verbal abuse. Terry would tell me I was too fat even though I was a size 0! Also, he would call me stupid and all kinds of mean words. Terry did not work. Meanwhile, I worked, made the meals and paid all the bills.

One time we were traveling to Hawaii for vacation. I had forgotten to bring along enough quarters for the luggage carts. Terry was so angry at me that he cussed me out in front of other people. I needed to pee and use the bathroom but he said I had to wait until we boarded the plane to go to the bathroom. I miserably waited the whole time until we boarded the plane. If this happened today I would have told him to go jump in a lake and went to the bathroom. Looking back now, I realized how much Terry controlled my life and I didn't fight back. Years of being told that I was fat, stupid, and ugly had taken its toll on my self-confidence. Strangely, I could be assertive at work but not with my husband. I told no one not even my family about this abuse.

    I knew something had to change. Terry agreed to a counselor at our church. Nothing changed. The counselor said Terry needed to help clean the house and Terry said the bathroom was not part of the house and he would not clean the toilet! One day Terry wrote this long letter to the head pastor at the mega church we attended. The Pastor called me into his office. I felt like I was being called into the Principal's office and I had done something wrong. Pastor shared with me the letter that Terry mailed to him. After talking for a few minutes, Pastor said that in his 30 years of being a Pastor that my marriage was the most dysfunctional marriage he had seen. Great! That is not the type of thing anyone wants to hear. He also, said that whatever my decision whether to stay with Terry or leave him that the church stood behind me. What a relief. I was raised that divorce is bad and should be avoided at all costs. Plus, Terry was telling me what a bad person I was because I was divorcing him even though he had already been married and divorced to his first wife. While I don't recommend divorce as the first step when your marriage is rocky but sometimes it is the only options. Especially, if you are being abused every day. My self-confidence was destroyed. Terry controlled everything even how much money we spent eating out even though I was the one paying!

    Finally, one day I had enough. Terry was driving to Nebraska to metal detect which was a hobby he enjoyed. Terry went out to his car and the tire was flat. He comes back into the house and demands the keys to my car so he can leave for

Nebraska. I was left without a car to drive to work and I had to ask a co-worker to give me a ride to work. I came home after work and no Terry. Eventually, around 9 pm Terry returned home. For the entire day, I was left without a car. The car which I paid for. This made me realize that Terry had no concern about me or my well-being. It was all about him. I exploded and lit into Terry and told him I had enough and we were getting a divorce. He begged and pleaded but my mind was made up.

Terry stretched out the divorce settlement for eight months. Basically, he took me to the cleaners since I had supported him for 10 years.

I was working in a stressful job supervising 20 employees at State Farm, going through a divorce, out of my home and family fighting. Some of the darkest days in my life. One verse that pulled me through was Jeremiah 29:11 "For I know the plans I have for you, declares the Lord, they are plans for good and not for evil, to give you a future and a hope." Every day I read this verse until it was embedded in my brain. Somehow I had to come through this dark time. This faith and hope that my life would get better kept me going.

LESSON LEARNED: Choose your mate carefully because this will impact you for the rest of your life. Even when you have a bad relationship still learn from the experience. You can choose to leave a bad situation. Don't stay stuck.

55

Boundaries

MY GIRLFRIEND, ROBIN, gave me a book, "Boundaries." At the time, I didn't know why she gave me this book. After reading the book realized that I did not have good boundaries. I allowed people to abuse me and I did not stop them. Especially, with Terry I did not stand up to him until the end of the marriage. Our marriage and relationship gradually deteriorated over time because I allowed others to treat me badly. Terry realized he could trample over me and get away with it. The "red flags" were there. He wanted me to limit how much I talked to my family, even though I was the one paying the phone bill. He constantly told me that I was overweight which at 95 pounds and a size 0 was too skinny. For instance, he did not want me to go out in public unless I was wearing makeup. Terry wanted me to dress a certain way. Also, how stupid I was. And that I needed to exercise more and be more fit. He wasn't so concerned about my health but rather because he thought it made me look more attractive. Terry was very superficial that way. He had gotten to the point where he would call me at work to swear at me over the phone telling me what I had done wrong.

LESSONS LEARNED: Know the signs of an abusive relationship. If someone does not respect you and controls your every move then that is not healthy. Be cautious of a charming person who often is a manipulator. And if you are in an abusive relationship then get the hell out. Ask for help and don't do this by yourself. Better to end a bad marriage than be treated like dirt. Respect yourself enough to stop abusive treatment.

56

Israel
HOPE IN THE STORM

DURING THE TIME I WAS SEPARATED from my husband I took a group trip to Israel with my Pastor from Resurrection Fellowship church. I had heard people say they felt closer to God and could feel His presence there. I thought that was a lot of baloney and people made this stuff up. Yet, I can say a couple of times I really felt like God was there with us. In particular, when we went into the jail where Jesus was kept before he was crucified. You had to go down steps and it was beneath ground. At that moment, I felt the presence of God.

Israel was a beautiful country. We visited the Dead Sea, Jerusalem, the Wailing Wall and Garden of Gethsemane. The food was delicious and a great break from my life.

Another beautiful moment was when we were in an ancient church and sang. The acoustics were glorious and we felt inspired.

LESSONS LEARNED: Traveling expands enriches your life. Learning about other cultures is wonderful. Sometimes, when life is crazy you need to "pause" life, change where you are at and get some perspective.

57

Mom's Alzheimer's & Family Fighting

IN ADDITION TO BEING SEPARATED, my family was fighting about my mom. My mom had Alzheimer's and she was deteriorating quickly. Mom was still living in her own home with my brother, Jon. My older brothers Paul and Jim thought she should be put into a nursing home. The question was what nursing home and what town? All my brothers lived in different cities. My brothers were calling me morning, noon, and night trying to get me to side with them. Finally, after weeks of this I said to stop calling me. I was already going through hell in my life going through the divorce from Terry. They decided to put my mom in a nursing home near my brother, Jim who lived in Eugene. He said that his daughters, my mom's grandchildren, could visit often. They didn't visit mom at all. It became apparent that my mom was being ignored. One time when my brother, Jon, was visiting mom they made their "escape" from the nursing home. Somehow, they walked out of there and Jon took Mom back to her home. She stayed there until it was apparent that she no longer knew where she was at and Jon found a nearby nursing home for Mom.

LESSONS LEARNED: Make plans for your family before it becomes a crisis. Then when you need to make a big decision everyone is in agreement. It is sad when families fight and work through the differences if possible.

58

My First Dog, Ahava

DURING THE WHOLE TIME I was married to Terry he never wanted a pet, not even a goldfish. So when we split up I got a puppy, Cocker Spaniel and named him Ahava which means "love." He was coal black, with wavy long hair. The most beautiful and sweetest dog ever. I loved this dog. He wanted to be with me and was unconditional in his love. Unfortunately, he has passed on now. Dogs are therapy.

LESSONS LEARNED: If someone doesn't love animals they have a hole in their heart. Dogs are therapy and unconditional love.

59

Leaving State Farm

MY MARRIAGE HAD ENDED. I was on to another adventure in my career. I left State Farm to start my own business in a direct sales company marketing wellness products. I thought I could do well in this and the corporate life was not for me anymore. After almost of year of running up credit card bills and not making any viable income I had to do something different. Lost my house and everything. All that I had was what I could fit into a small VW Bug.

Was this leap into the unknown a big adventure or failure? At the time, I felt like a huge failure. Here was a college educated, professional with no home and no career. I did find a basement apartment to rent for a short time. I take responsibility for my actions. Realized I should have swallowed my pride and asked for help much sooner but thought I could do this on my own.

Later on this big failure turns into a blessing.

LESSON LEARNED: When you are "drowning" call out for help and the helpers will be there. Also, "count the cost" when deciding to make the leap. Look at the pros and cons and have an escape route. Calculate the risks of gains or losses.

60

Back to Oregon

AT THIS TIME, Mom was deteriorating quickly with Alzheimer. Every time I called she could not talk on the phone. My brother, Jon was her caretaker. I had nothing holding me in Colorado.

I drove back to Oregon in my VW Bug and stayed at my mom's house with my brother. By this time mom was in a nursing home. Jon and I would go to visit her often. It was so sad because she did not know who we were and could not talk anymore. Mom even did not enjoy eating. I would bring her flowers and it meant nothing to her. Heartbreaking how she had become a shell of herself.

One day Mom passed on. We were sad but relieved. Mom was in such a terrible state that I could not bear to see her that way any longer.

LESSONS LEARNED: Make time for your loved ones. You don't know how many days you each have.

61

Back to Colorado

AFTER MY MOM PASSED AWAY, I had no reason to stay in Oregon. I realized that I had friends, great church and loved Colorado. Packed up my car, I drove back to Colorado. I had kept my insurance license it was easy to find a job. I worked in various agent's offices filling in when they were shorthanded.

I was doing the same job that I had done when I was 17 years old and working as a secretary in an insurance agent's office. But, I had to work and State Farm was not hiring. Even if they were hiring I don't think that I would enjoy working in that corporate environment again.

My girlfriend owned a rental house in Old Town Fort Collins which I rented from her. It was a great place and walking distance to downtown. Had an enclosed front porch and garden area in the backyard.

LESSONS LEARNED: Starting over is not the end of the world. Humble yourself. Sometimes you do what you have to do to put food on the table.

62

Meeting Mike

MIKE AND I are a "Match" success story. The first week, I was back in Colorado I started dating Mike. When, I was single I had made a list of what I wanted in the next husband. Mike met 90% of those things on the list. I was even as specific as to the height, hair color and eye color.

On our first date was at Crazy Jacks. I was dressed in a sparkly blouse and jeans. Mike wore a ball cap, t-shirt and jeans. My first impression was that he didn't go out of his way to dress up. After about 15 minutes, Mike said he had to go home and check on his dogs. Again, I was not very impressed. Maybe he was checking to make sure that I didn't have horns and a tail! I don't know. But, I remember a girlfriend said to give a person at least a couple of dates to get to know them better. I gave Mike another chance and we went on a second date. That date went much better. We went to listen to live music and ate dinner at Crazy Jacks.

Mike said in his bio on Match that he was a "graphic writer" which I did not know what that was for sure. Did he write X rated material? Mike did show me a comic book that he said he wrote. Later on I went to a comic-book store and asked them if a Mike Baron wrote comics? They pulled out a book from the shelf and showed me one that he wrote. He had passed test one. That he did what he said he did.

Then, I did a search on the county records for any registered sex offenders. Mike was not on any of those lists. So far, so good. A girl cannot be too careful.

After only a few months of dating, we knew we were going to get married. Mike being more traditional waited until we had dated one year before he proposed to me He got down on one knee, with his dogs around him and pulled out a beautiful diamond engagement ring and proposed. I very happily accepted.

We had a beautiful wedding where we each wrote our vows. Mike wrote the script for our wedding. Our friend, Bruce, married us. It was a small wedding at a friend's house. Then, at the reception an Elvis impersonator serenaded the guests.

LESSONS LEARNED: Don't judge a book by its cover. And don't go for the "type" you always go for. Sometimes going against the type of guy or gal you think you want there may be a diamond in the rough. That is my husband, Mike. He is the type of person that the better you get to know him the more you like him. He has character, honesty and is damn funny!

63

Insurance Agent
THINGS ARE LOOKING UP

THERE WAS A JOB OPENING at Western Insurance Services for an insurance agent. I applied and did not think they would hire me but they did. The best part of this job was that I helped educate the policyholders on their policy coverage. I made sure they did not have too much or not enough coverage. The job was going well and my boss was happy.

During the day, I would work with customers and make sales calls. One day each week, I would go out and make "cold calls" to businesses in the local area. Other insurance agents were great referrals and I kept an ongoing contact with them through thank you cards.

One agent who was a great resource and support was Eric Weedin. Even though we did not refer to each other, Eric was always a great resource. He knew so much more than I did about Commercial insurance. I valued his expertise and willingness to help.

The big drawback was that the pay was low and I worked by myself doing everything. At the one year mark, I asked for a pay raise. My boss said they could not afford to give me more money (even though they were owned by a big bank). At that moment, I decided to look for another job.

LESSONS LEARNED: Have more confidence in yourself. You have more to offer than you know. Also, respect yourself. If others are not valuing you and paying accordingly then recognize this. People will only treat you the way you allow them to treat you.

64

Loveland Chamber
MY DREAM JOB

As I looked around for a new job, I saw a posting for salesperson for the Loveland Chamber. I did not think I was qualified but applied anyway. I had been a member and an Ambassador of this chamber for years so I already knew many of the members.

After applying for the job the rigorous hiring process started. First of all, I had to put together a business plan of how to grow the chamber and also retain members. I put together a plan and gave it to the Chamber President. Then, I was given a list of three businesses to contact and I was to give a report back of how that went. I contacted all three of the businesses. Two were located in Loveland so I could go to the business in person. In addition, I was given an assessment test. Then, I was interviewed by the owners at Sandler Training. This dragged on for over a month. They had gone through a couple of membership directors and wanted to make sure that they made the right choice. Brian had said he was going to make a decision at a certain time but I did not hear from him. Then, the next day I went to his office. He was in an appointment and I waited until his appointment was done. When I met with Brian he said he was still deciding. At this point, I said to him he needed to give me a "yes" or a "no" now and I wasn't going away until he made his decision. Finally, he realized I was serious about getting the job and that I would be assertive enough for the job.

Finally, I was in a job that I loved. I thrived and succeeded. My boss supported me but was not hovering over me. Enjoyed working with professionals and networking. Everything was going so well. Married, dream job and happiest I had been in a long time.

Many people said that I was one of the top salespeople that the Chamber ever had. I was making great connections. Also, I was able to use my creative ideas on how to improve and grow the chamber.

My goal was to help businesses grow. I did this through talking with the members and being a resource. I also did prospecting and cold calling. In addition, at events I concentrated on welcoming each member at the event. If I saw a "wall flower" and someone by themselves then I made a point to go over and talk with them. Plus, I introduced them to another professional who would be good for them to meet. I kept positive and looked for ways to serve.

When I was hired at the Chamber, Eric Weedin asked to quote my insurance. Since he had been a friend and professional support for many years then I was glad to have him do this. He was able to give me better coverage for about the same price. Plus, I trusted Eric's knowledge and integrity. This is where keeping contact with other professionals was rewarded.

Then, my boss got a job in another town. The chamber hired a new President. It was time to move on and I did. Broke my heart to leave the dream job but I knew I needed to do something different. Life goes on and so did I.

LESSONS LEARNED: Risk and take that leap of faith. Even if you don't think you will get the job still go for it. You never know until you try. Put others first. When a season in life ends then recognize the end of that time and move on.

65

Semi-Retired

AT THIS TIME, my husband was the breadwinner. Mike is a successful writer and I did not need to work. I enjoyed listing items on eBay. Also, I ran a free woman's networking group called Business Divas. It kept me in touch with other professionals but it wasn't stressful.

Basically, I had to grieve the loss of my dream job at the Chamber. During this time, I realized that my self-image is not in my job title or income. My whole life I was always striving for a better job and more income.

This time was introspection and healing. I went to Grief Counseling to help me sort out all the losses of family and work. One of the best things I did. I realized that I was not alone. Also, grief is not only over the loss of someone but also the loss of a dream.

LESSONS LEARNED: You are not your job title, car you drive, or money you make. Take time to pause and work through grief. Grief can pile up until it weighs you down and until you deal with this grief you cannot move on.

66
Cataract Surgery

MY EYESIGHT HAD BEEN DETERIORATING and I thought that I needed to have new eyeglasses. The eye doctor did his battery of tests. Then, he said I have good news and bad news. The bad news is that you have cataracts. The good news is that you can have cataract surgery. Since I had bad eyes my whole life I wasn't too surprised. It did make me nervous having surgery on my eyes but Mike had his cataract surgery the year before. His surgery went well.

Surgery day. Mike drove me to the new, surgery center. The clean and immaculate rooms helped calm me. The medical staff checked my blood pressure and explained the procedure. They wheeled me into the surgery room and moved me to a cold, metal operating table. Soon I was drifting off into half sleep yet still aware of the operation but I could not feel anything. In only a few minutes, the surgery was completed and I was returned to a private room. Almost immediately I could see better out of the eye they performed the surgery on. This was a miracle. Every day of my life I woke up and could barely see anything. Now, when I wake up I can see!

The second eye was operated on a couple of weeks later. To this day, it was one of the best things that have happened to me. No more glasses or contacts.

LESSONS LEARNED: What may sound like bad news can turn into good.

67

Northern Colorado Community
STARTING MY OWN BUSINESS

AFTER RUNNING THE BUSINESS DIVAS NETWORKING group for professional women for free I had an "aha" moment. What if I charged a small membership and started a networking group for men and women. Ran it by a couple of my professional friends who said they were wondering when I would do that and encouraged me to start the group. Therefore, Northern Colorado Community began over four years ago. At my first event 42 people showed up. In the first month several members joined. Gradually over the years the group grew.

I offered speakers at lunch and learns. In addition, we had business after hours and masterminds. I contacted my professional contacts to host or speak. The attendance at the after-hours grew to 20-40 attendees. The lunch and learns were having 20-40 attendees too. Folks said they felt welcomed and were growing their business.

My goal with the group is to have a "community" of professionals where each person felt important. In addition, I did "high touch" activities such as a 1-on-1 new member meeting. Taking the time to really get to know the member and connecting them to other professionals through introduction emails. Each new member received a handmade card that I made and mailed to them. Over time, I added one free hour each month in consulting services with me. Each member could access resources, connections, and inclusion in my group.

At this point, I have 70 members. Everyone from Blue Federal Credit Union to solo entrepreneurs such as Compustar IT. I found my place.

LESSONS LEARNED: Build it and they will come. If you have already built a good reputation then when you do start a new businesspeople are more open to listening. Keep in contact with professionals. Stay visible.

68

Ordinary Extraordinary People Awards Banquet

ONE DAY THE THOUGHT CAME TO ME to put together a banquet recognizing the "Go Givers" and little recognized people who give back to the local community. They may be volunteers, stay at home moms, board members and other who daily give of their time and resources. There was no such award like this recognizing the everyday person who makes other lives better and they do this on their own. I had coffee with my girlfriend, Deb, who had a lot of event experience. I said to her this may be a crazy idea but this is what I was thinking. She said do it and she would help me in any way she could. The first year we had over 20 nominations from the local community. We recognized three men and three women who give back to the local community. I had a nomination, review committee who narrowed it down to 12 nominees. Put it out for a public vote to narrow down to the top six honorees. We had an elegant banquet in 2018 and I felt inspired. There were folks I did not know who were doing so much to make this a better place. That began the banquet and I did one in 2019 as well. Many people came up to me later and said how inspired and wonderful this awards banquet was to them. One of the honorees in 2019 has since passed away. He shared with me that receiving this award was the highlight of his year. Now, in retrospect, I am so glad he was one of the honorees.

Lessons learned: Stretch yourself to do what you think is impossible. There always needs to be ways to recognize others and inspire others. You never know when the person you honored may no longer be with us and you took the time to recognize their life.

69
COVID

FOR MONTHS, I watched You Tube videos of COVID hitting other countries. What happened and the drastic impact. When the first case hit Colorado, I said to my husband we need to get groceries today. And especially, toilet paper. Who knew that toilet paper would become such a hot product and in short supply? Within a few days no one could find toilet paper or hand sanitizer. It was crazy. People were in a daze and shock.

I had been running my business for over three years and year four was going to be my "banner" year. Momentum was built up and lots of folks had heard of my group. Then COVID happened in March 2020. Everything was shut down including group events. For the first week, I cried. Something like this had never happened during my lifetime. The only stores open were the essential ones such as grocery stores and home improvement. Even craft stores were closed.

In my networking business, Northern Colorado Community I had to make major adjustments. I started using Zoom to have meetings online. Not as good as in person but better than doing nothing. Also, I started mailing out one card a day to my members. A way to keep in touch and let them know that I was thinking about them. I would call or drop off a small gift to a member's office.

Gradually, businesses and group gatherings were allowed. I had a small group get together outside at a local business. Folks were so starved for in person networking. The term of "social distancing" was used a lot but I rather call it "physical distancing." We are social beings and we were created to interact and have relationships.

What was so sad during this time is grandparents who couldn't hug their grand kids. Or businesses who had been in business a long time closing up shop. I did my best to support local businesses.

I was sad that I could not have the banquet for the Ordinary Extraordinary People award since large groups could not gather. Many nonprofits could not have their normal in person fund raising banquets. Instead, everything went online or did not happen at all.

LESSONS LEARNED: Don't take things or people for granted. I can adjust with drastic changes and not crumble.

70

ShoppingNoCo

WHEN I SAW that the online shopping was growing I offered a website where small businesses could get listed called ShoppingNoCo. This was successful because it gathered the small businesses under one website and gave them some leverage against the "Big Box Stores." Simply another way to support small businesses.

LESSONS LEARNED: Think creatively about what small businesses want or need. It may not be the standard way of doing business. Then offer that service or product

71

2020: A Year of Adjustment

OVER THE YEAR 2020 we have all had to learn how to adjust and cope. For me one way I learned to cope was being creative. Creativity flowed in my card making and mixed media art. Cooking is another creative outlet which I enjoyed learning and doing more baking.

During this time, I started baking. For the first time in my life, I baked bread. Actually, the bread turned out well. Then, I went on to baking pies. Baked pies for friends who said they were delicious.

Learned new art techniques. I continued making cards and sending a card to one of my members each day to keep in touch with them.

LESSONS LEARNED: Life can change drastically in a flash. Learn who are your true friends and keep in contact with them. I communicated with my family on a more regular basis through phone calls, letters and Zoom. Your health is very important when fighting any possible disease. Fur babies are very important and therapeutic. Be grateful for what your blessings. Slow down and value each day.

72
2021

WE ALL HAVE HIGH HOPES for the New Year. I am planning my events. Looking back on what I learned. Writing my autobiography and planning ahead.

Slowly things are opening up and I am having small networking events. Many events are outdoors when the weather is good. Folks are starved for making connections. My main goal for my business in 2021 is to continue the support for the members and being a resource for them.

I continue to keep in touch with my family. I flew out to Oregon in February and had a great visit. Also, still doing the Zoom calls with my family. Realizing how important your loved ones are to you. It takes extra work to keep connected but it is important.

LESSONS LEARNED: Remember, what is important. Even if extra work keep in touch with your friends and family.

73

What I Would Tell My Younger Self

WHAT WOULD I TELL MY YOUNGER SELF now that I am nearing the mature age of 60?

Life does not turn out how you planned it. Stop being disappointed when life does not go as planned. There are many dips and turns in the road of life. When I was growing up I always thought I wanted to be a teacher. Then I was a teacher and I hated it. Actually, I loved the creative elements of teaching but not all the politics and side issues.

Be brave and take that leap into the unknown. The best surprises were when I went ahead and jumped into something I knew nothing about and actually loved. For instance, I applied at a job at the Loveland Chamber and had no background in that type of work. I had worked in the insurance industry for 20 years. What did I know of the chamber world? I absolutely loved being there for small businesses and the business development.

When life crushes you there is still only YOU! You are still the important part of your life. Not your job title, fancy house, income or even friends. The internal, gutsy core of you is still there. You may feel like you have "disappeared" or want to die but the essence of what you are about is still there and has been all along.

Failure is not the end but steppingstones in life. I have had many "steppingstones" times in my life, finances, marriage, and career. At that time, my life seemed a total and doomed failure. How could the honor roll and smart student fail so miserably? It is that scraping myself up from the bottom and going out to another day called real life. Realizing life goes on and you either have to pull yourself up or be stuck in eternal depression. I chose to pull myself up.

Choose your mate wisely. The first time I married was terrible. I married a narcissistic and bi-polar man who abused me. After several years I had enough. Then many years as a single person I met a wonderful person who is now my husband, Mike. He was nothing like what I thought I wanted but someone I cherish and love dearly. Mike has integrity, grit, kindness and funny as hell.

Surround yourself with strong, confident and encouraging friends. Sometimes women find someone who clings to them or is downright mean. You don't need those type of friends. You will in time ferret out the true and loyal friends who want the best for you and support you through your adventures. Again, choose friends wisely.

Most of all, value and appreciate each day which is a gift from God.

LESSONS LEARNED: Life may not turn out the way you expect but dust yourself off and take one step at a time. Learn from the mistakes and don't stay in the mire. Move forward each day.

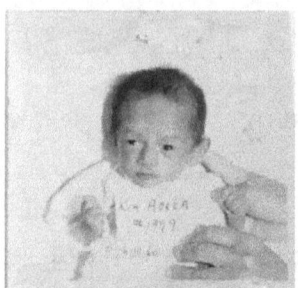

Ann as a baby in the orphanage when first found

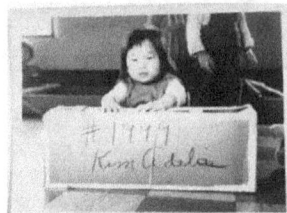

Ann (4 yrs old) in orphanage before flying to US

Ann in grade school

Ann with brothers Jim & Paul

Ann with Paul, Jim & Jon

Family photo of all siblings & spouses — Back Row: Jon, Christine, Jim & Barb; Front Row: Ann, Paul & Leslie

Dad, Von Brenner   *Mom & dad, Von & Betty Brenner*

Mom & brother, Jon

Ann & her mom, Betty Brenner

Ann at her naturalization

Ann's Senior H.S. photo

High School graduation

Family photo with Mom, brothers & brother's spouse & children

Mike and Ann's wedding photo

Ann in South Korea wearing a traditional, Korean dress

Ann with the group of adoptees & guides on the "Motherland" tour

Puppies, Bob, Mack & Freddy

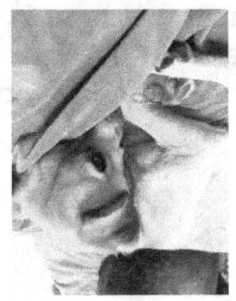
The youngest puppy, Freddy

Acknowledgements:

First of all, I want to recognize my parents who adopted me. They gave me a chance for a new and wonderful life. Also, thank you to my biological Mom who chose to give me life. Even though she did not keep me she knew that some family out there could give me a loving home. I will never know who she is but grateful for that original life giving decision she made.

Thank you to my husband, Mike, who has been there for me and always wants the best for me. He was my editor for this book as well. I love you, Mike.

In addition, all my friends and family who were there for me and rooted me on. Plus, the professionals who trusted me with their time and resources by joining as a member of Northern Colorado Community.

Most of all to God who gave me life and purpose. I am grateful there is someone bigger than myself who I can have faith and trust in them. When times were scary my faith in God was my rock.

About the Author:

I live in Colorado with my husband and three "fur babies" or puppies. The puppies names are Bob, Freddy and Mack. My husband, Mike Baron, is an award winning writer. He has written many comic books and several novels. Colorado has wonderful scenery and a great place to live. In my spare time, I enjoy making cards. This autobiography is the first book that I have written. I hope you have enjoyed the book and you were inspired.

RESOURCE PAGE:

Link to Holt Adoption:
https://www.holtinternational.org/

Post Adoption Services for Adoptees:
https://www.holtinternational.org/pas/for-adoptees/

Resources for adoptees:
https://www.holtinternational.org/pas/adoptee/adoptee-resources/

Films about adoption: https://harlows-monkey.com/resources/films/

Korean American website:
http://koreanamericanstory.org/

My business website:
https://northerncoloradocommunity.com/

Article written about me in Voyage Denver:
https://shoutoutcolorado.com/meet-ann-baron-ceo-founder/

Podcast interview about my business:
https://anchor.fm/loco-think-tank/episodes/SHORTS-14--Ann-Baron--Creating-Community-in-Northern-Colorado-esrrrd

Article by BizWest about how businesses adjusted during Pandemic. I was one of the businesses interviewed: https://bizwest.com/2020/05/28/work-life-balance-shifts-in-response-to-pandemic/

Article about me in magazine Regenerate:
http://regeneratemagazine.com/2018/04/know-sure-now-3/

www.ingramcontent.com/pod-product-compliance
Lightning Source LLC
Chambersburg PA
CBHW072010290426
44109CB00018B/2192